920.7
B7345w **Brannum, Mary,** 1938–
    When I was 16; by Mary Brannum and the editors.
Photos. by Camilla Smith. New York, Platt & Munk ₍1967₎

    318 p. ports. 23 cm.

68–97

    1. Women in the U. S.—Biog.   I. Title.

CT3260.B75   920.073   67–22933

                                                  395
Library of Congress   ₍5₎

When I was 16

When I was 16

by Mary Brannum and the Editors

Photographs by Camilla Smith

PLATT & MUNK, *Publishers* / NEW YORK

Introduction

"What were you like at sixteen?" There were, it seemed to the editors, good reasons for asking this question of eighteen notable women and for hoping that their response would be meaningful. For a girl especially, sixteen is a time of transition—from tomboy to young lady, from gawkiness to grace. It is intriguing to be given a glimpse of this fleeting time. Sixteen is also a turning point between childhood and maturity. What determines the choices that are made? Is it wayward chance or deep conviction that leads one person to become a movie star, another a poet? There is fascination, too, in having people remember themselves at an age when they were vulnerable, less sure, less knowing. In the process, we see aspects of their personalities that are not often revealed.

Some of the women in *When I Was 16* are more famous than

others, but all have achieved distinction. (In this sense, the book illustrates the variety of careers open to a girl of sixteen, many more today than when most of the women in this book were young.) Because they are distinguished women, however, interviewing them presented some problems. All are involved in life beyond the purely domestic circle. They are eminently modern and busy (some wished they were less so), and their time for projects like this one is limited. Another difficulty was this: a strange person comes to see you and asks you to bare your soul and then to allow it to be printed in a book. Conscience, confidences of friends and the laws of libel, of course, had a restricting effect on what each person said.

Still, what they did say is remarkably informative. They talked about a year in their lives that is ordinarily left out of history books, and did so in a detailed, entertaining way. Quite naturally, they also related what happened at sixteen to what came before and what followed, commenting on a variety of topics and putting the sixteenth year in the perspective of a lifetime.

The response was warm. They gave themselves over readily, and often with delight, to being sixteen for a few hours. Reminiscences, hopes, embarrassments, questions and curiosities and longings were recalled with enthusiasm. There was great spontaneity. As Marianne Moore has written elsewhere, "the rhythm of speech is the rhythm of a person."

Sixteen is often a year of realization, not necessarily decisive but always strongly felt and remembered. "I stood on a lonely road at sunset and thought it was the end of everything," said Margaret Mead. The sense of change and the strength of feeling that come with being sixteen can be stunning and freeing at the same time. Reading about it, the editors hope, will show how right Brenda Ueland was when she said: "Well, let it come. We are open to things."

Contents

7   *Introduction*

15   Marietta Tree

36   Suzanne Farrell

52   Sandra Hochman

68   Eileen Ford

85   Margaret Mead

100   Bette Davis

113   Gloria Foster

134   Marisa Berenson

147   Mary S. Calderone, M.D.

168   Betsey Johnson

Contents

188   Mary Dublin Keyserling

200   Frances Scott Fitzgerald Lanahan

218   Marianne Moore

232   Ruth Fuller, M.D

251   Sybil Christopher

270   Jacquelyn Anderson Mattfeld

287   Brenda Ueland

308   Mrs. Lyndon Baines Johnson

When I was 16

Marietta Tree

Marietta Tree's New England family has a tradition of devo-tion to causes, in particular to those concerned with religion, education and social welfare.

Her father, the Reverend Malcolm E. Peabody, is a retired Episcopal Bishop of Central New York and a Harvard Over-seer. Her mother, Mary, always active in community service, was put in jail in 1964 for taking part in a civil rights demonstration in the South.

Born April 12, 1917, in Lawrence, Massachusetts, Mary Endicott Peabody was an only girl among four brothers. She often visited her paternal grandparents in Groton, Massachu-setts. Much the same quiet New England atmosphere prevailed there as at home in Lawrence, except that in Groton there were more boys: Marietta's grandfather, Endicott Peabody, was founder and for many years headmaster of Groton School.

Her schooling was varied and extensive: she attended Shady Hill School, Chestnut Hill, Pennsylvania; St. Timothy's, Catonsville, Maryland; La Petite École Florentine, Florence, Italy; and the University of Pennsylvania. She studied political science at the University, and earned expense money by working as a model in a Philadelphia department store.

In 1939 she married Desmond Fitzgerald, a young lawyer. With World War II, he went into the army, and she worked for the office of the coordinator of Inter-American Affairs and as a researcher on Life *magazine. They had one daughter, Frances, and in 1947 they were divorced.*

Later that year, she married Arthur Ronald Lambert Field Tree, a British investment banker who had been a member of Parliament for thirteen years. They have one daughter, Penelope. During the first two years of their marriage they lived in England, then came to the United States, where Mrs. Tree again became active in interracial community work in New York City. (In 1944 she had helped found Sydenham Hospital, the first interracial voluntary hospital in the United States.)

Mrs. Tree first entered active Democratic politics as a volunteer researcher and speech-writer at Democratic State Committee headquarters. After attending the 1952 Democratic National Convention, she joined Volunteers for Stevenson.

In 1954 she managed Anthony B. Akers' campaign for election to Congress from a New York City district. She rushed from a banquet honoring Britain's Queen Mother, Elizabeth, to her candidate's headquarters on election night, only to see him defeated. Mrs. Tree did not lose her enthusiasm for politics, however. She was among the leaders of the Volunteers for Stevenson organization in New York City in 1956, and in 1958 she again worked for Akers for Congress. In 1960 she was Vice-chairman of the Citizens' Committee for Kennedy.

[16]

When John F. Kennedy became President, he appointed Mrs. Tree to the post of U.S. Representative to the U.N. Commission on Human Rights, and from 1961 to 1965 she worked at the U.S. Mission to the United Nations. In 1964 President Johnson appointed her Representative to the U.N. Trusteeship Council with the personal rank of Ambassador. This made her America's first woman Ambassador to the United Nations. In 1965 she became the Secretary-General's Personal Representative to the U.N. International School, and, in November, 1966, she was elected a delegate-at-large to the New York State Constitutional Convention.

Mrs. Tree continues to be active in civil rights and in international affairs. She is presently a director of the Institute of International Education, the U.N. Association, the National Committee Against Discrimination in Housing, the African-American Institute and the Asia Society.

Marietta Tree

Marietta tree's office is on the eighth floor of the United Nations Secretariat. A spacious, quiet room, it is pleasant after the noise and bustle of the corridor outside: brown leather chairs and a couch bright with orange pillows, a large clean desk, sunlight shining through the windows over one wall.

In the center of the room and like its chief decoration stood Mrs. Tree, wearing a well-cut beige suit and white blouse. She smiled at me from an imposing height of five feet ten inches. "Excuse me," she said, apologetically swallowing a peppermint lozenge, "I have a terrible cold." She paced about a little, then sat back in the couch, resting her honey-blond head on it and crossing her long, slim legs in a movement which I later discovered was her thinking posture. She began to speak in a husky, measured voice.

"The other day I read some diaries I kept when I was a teenager, and I was appalled at how naive I was then. I'm not sure that my values were terribly good when I was sixteen.

What I mean is that I was awfully frivolous and gay—thought about parties and dances all the time. I thought, of course, that I was a very serious person, but most of my waking moments were spent at parties. It wasn't until I was forced to go to college that I began to really read, to lead a daytime life.

"Of course, I had been away to school before—boarding school in Maryland—and I was delighted to go, very grateful to have the chance to be judged for myself alone and not according to the achievements of my family. Then, too, I had four younger brothers at home. Perhaps I was in some sort of competition with them for my parents' attention.

"The year I was sixteen, my last year at St. Timothy's, I was captain of the Brownie team. The whole school was divided into two teams for hockey and basketball, the Brownies and the Spiders, and it was more than just rivalry on the hockey field or the basketball court. It was supposed to be a whole way of life, and I took it seriously. I remember I used to wake up my team members before 6:30 in the morning to make them practice. Now that I think of it, I drove those poor girls mercilessly. It seems unbelievable now, but it was a deadly serious thing at the time."

I asked Mrs. Tree if the Brownies had won that year. She grinned and nodded, stretching her leg out in front of her. "Luckily for me. I suppose in some ways it was the crowning achievement of my sixteenth year. And, do you know, I've never been especially good at sports since then. Oh, I enjoy tennis and golf (even though I've given up golf—I hate having to belong to a club in order to play), but I'm really rather a mediocre sportswoman. Now I can shudder at the thought of making those girls get up before dawn to practice their hockey strokes and basketball plays.

"My grandmother, I remember, was tremendously athletic.

She used to ride every day and had what was called then a beautiful seat. We took up golf together when I was sixteen. She was in her early seventies, but she was beautifully coordinated and she beat me right away. She was a great idol of mine. I was the oldest of her grandchildren, and she had the unique quality of making each of us feel treasured and prized. When any of us was away she would write us long, wonderful letters. She was a great extrovert, partly because she was married to the headmaster of a boys' school. She remembered the name of each boy and everything about him. She was a tremendously loving person.

"My other grandmother was different. She was a great beauty and a marvelous flirt. I used to have trouble holding on to my beaux around her. She was an intellectual and a passionate woman. She not only had ideas—she cared about them and did something about them. I remember that I would come home from dances in Boston and find her translating a Russian novel into Greek or something of the sort. I guess in a way my two grandmothers, each of them unique and quite wonderful, were my two real heroines at the time.

"The headmistress at St. Timothy's was also a great influence on me then, though not precisely a heroine. She was very strict, almost medieval. She had precise ideas about rules and regulations, and about life.

"Another woman who influenced me was a teacher I had, a Miss Elmore. To my everlasting gratitude, she taught me to appreciate poetry. She was a frail little woman who loved poetry with her heart and soul. I remember she used to throw back her head and actually bellow when she was reading certain passages from Shakespeare. She was marvelous! I was very romantic at the time. I had fallen in love with *War and Peace* and I was fascinated and terrified by *The Brothers*

Karamazov, but Miss Elmore was the one who really made poetry live for me. I became poetry-drenched. So many young people now have poetry ruined for them by unimaginative teachers who approach it stodgily and take all the beauty from it. Miss Elmore was a romantic, and that's what it takes to reach students.

"I don't mean to give the impression that I was all soulful and profound at the time. I existed, the year I was sixteen, to go to dances and football games and parties. Being popular and sought-after was extremely important. I know I always appeared confident, socially, but of course I wasn't. I don't think anyone ever is. There are always doubts. My friends used to tell me how confident I seemed, but secretly I knew that I had an advantage. My grandfather was, after all, headmaster of a boys' school, and I knew more boys than anyone in my class. At dances, of course, they felt obligated to dance with me. For all my seeming confidence, I was in despair about my appearance. I think the fact that I had succeeded in my own little world, being captain of the Brownie team, helped me immensely. No one could imagine the turmoil going on within me about the way I looked."

Mrs. Tree stood up and got a cigarette, moving with such grace that it was hard to imagine she had ever worried about her appearance. She coughed slightly and tossed her head. In that instant she seemed sixteen. "Yes, *despair,*" she said as she took her seat. "I was five foot ten by the time I was fourteen. That's very painful. I remember my father used to imitate me on the dance floor. He would waltz around—to the laughter of my mother and my four younger brothers—with his shoulders all tucked in and his head at an odd angle. He was right, of course. I can remember dancing cheek-to-cheek with boys with my behind all stuck out to try to appear smaller. I used to kind of crouch on the dance floor in the hopes of minimizing my height. But all that did was make it more apparent. No matter how many times you're told height will be an asset later on in life you never believe it.

"Since boys don't grow as quickly as girls, it was a terrible problem, and it used to sadden me that my father didn't realize how painful it was for me to be five ten. I suppose I would have given anything to be small. Then, too, I had a slight skin problem. That's an endless vicious cycle. It's brought on by being tense about things—studies or boys or whatever. The tenser you get, the worse the skin problem becomes. I think it comes from the intense inner problem of 'Who am I?' It is so difficult to know who you are at that age, at least it was for me, and you worry and worry until you have created an inescapable trap of inadequacy.

"When I was sixteen I hadn't the slightest idea of my own identity. It seems to me that this generation is so much more well-informed and confident than mine was. My daughters and their friends have very good ideas of who they are. They've read books and they can discuss things and in general they make good companions. They dress well and know how to make the most of their assets, which are considerable. I don't know why it is, but they seem to have an extraordinary sense of self which was completely lacking when I was sixteen.

"Take grades, for example. When I first entered college, it was considered a great handicap to have a brain. I remember very well entering a dance in my freshman year and hearing a girl who was supposed to be a friend of mine saying: 'Oh! There's Marietta. *She's* intelligent. *She* goes to college!' Of course, that was supposed to ruin me with the boys that evening, absolutely destroy me.

"My daughters are proud when they get good grades. The

life of the mind is no longer something at which one sneers. That in itself is a great advance and definitely a part of what makes this new generation so much more aware of themselves as important members of society. They use their minds and are always expanding.

"I'm ashamed to say that my heroes at that time were not necessarily 'men of great ideas.' I idolized Duke Ellington, who is still a great hero of mine, and Leslie Howard and another British actor named Robert Donat. They were marvelous, and I can still appreciate them today. But the point is, my mind was attuned to idolizing bandleaders and actors rather than political figures.

"Which is especially strange because I had the great good fortune of knowing Franklin Roosevelt. I met him in 1931 or 1932, when he was Governor of New York. He had gone to Groton and remained devoted to the school. He came back to Groton in September that year, and there were a whole lot of us grandchildren there. I must have been about fourteen at the time. Being the oldest, I was the lucky one who got to sit next to him at dinner. I remember his enormous charm. He put me completely at ease as he asked me questions, what I enjoyed doing, about my school and about my cousins sitting around the table. He made me feel my company was worthwhile, that I was a person, not a child.

"He was very fond of my grandfather and grandmother, and he came back again the next year. I sat next to him again and, do you know, he remembered everything I had told him the year before: the names of my younger cousins and where they went to school—everything! And it wasn't a trick. He was genuinely interested, which I think accounts for a great part of his enormous success.

"Now for the amazing part of all this. When I was sixteen

Roosevelt was elected President. In spite of having met him twice before, in spite of having been completely charmed by him and enormously impressed, I was the leader of the forces for Hoover at school. I can't imagine for the life of me how I was able to do that. Obviously knowing Franklin Roosevelt at that age had an enormous effect on me, and yet I wasn't able to campaign for him at school." Mrs. Tree shook her head and looked at her hands.

"You see, my parents were staunch Republicans, as were all the people I met when I was growing up in Philadelphia. They actually thought the Republic would crack apart if a Democrat were elected President. That must have been it. I let the prejudices of my environment overcome my real knowledge. It just goes to prove how feeble one is in one's judgment at that age, how little I was able to believe in myself and trust in myself. I just went along with what others thought, as if my own feelings couldn't matter very much. I can't imagine many sixteen-year-olds behaving that way today. My daughter and her friends have very definite personal feelings and a great integrity about them. They trust their ability to formulate opinions. I didn't, obviously. I was so, well, unformed, I suppose you could say.

"I had a great fantasy world, but I'm afraid it's rather difficult to remember precisely what it was all about. I know I thought a great deal about going on the stage, becoming an actress. We had plays at school, mostly Shakespeare. I enjoyed acting enormously. One year I played Ariel in *The Tempest* and another year Bottom in *A Midsummer Night's Dream.* Actually I had great dreams of becoming a blues singer"—she looked at the ceiling—"I had a picture of myself in a black dress singing sad songs in a blue spotlight."

Had she ever confided these ambitions, especially the one

[25]

about torch singing, to anyone? "Well, I shouldn't think so. They're rather embarrassing to admit even now, don't you think?"

Just as I was about to tell her that I thought she'd make a terrific blues singer, her secretary came in and said there was a phone call. When she answered, her voice sounded spontaneously glad to hear whoever it was on the other end.

Afterwards, she returned to the couch, paused, then continued: "Oddly enough, I did have a chance to act a number of years later. In 1960, after the convention in Los Angeles, I went to Reno to see an old friend, John Huston. For years he had been after me to come and see a film in the making, but I had never been able to. He was shooting *The Misfits,* starring Marilyn Monroe and Clark Gable, and the first day I was there John took me to various meetings, with the chief cameraman and with Arthur Miller, who had written the screenplay. I was absolutely fascinated by it all. Suddenly I found myself in a room where Clark Gable was interviewing local actresses for a small part. He had spoken with one or two, then suddenly he turned to me—I was sitting quietly in a corner—and pointed. 'I think I'll take *you* for the part,' he said. I thanked him and assured him I wasn't an actress. But he just laughed and said, 'Oh, honey, it's the easiest thing in the world. Just stand up and we'll go through the lines right here.'

"Then John Huston went through them with me five or six or maybe even ten times, and the next morning at eight we filmed the scene down at the railroad station in Reno. I played a girl who had just gotten a divorce in Reno, and Clark Gable was a cowboy who worked on a divorce ranch. He was seeing me off, and trying to make it as painless and quick as possible. We were able to do the scene in one take. I'm told that's unusual.

"The next day we had to go down to the station again to take some still photos from all angles. Our positions had been chalked out for us, and we had to stand, noses practically touching, while we talked about things you normally stand four feet apart to discuss. 'I have a fifteen-year-old stepson,' said Mr. Gable, an inch away from me. 'Do you think I should send him to military school?' Then we discussed hunting dogs. My husband was interested in hunting dogs, so we had a conversation about them while they shot these pictures. If anyone had told me when I was sixteen that I'd be standing nose to nose with Clark Gable on a station platform in Reno discussing hunting dogs I would have thought they were mad.

"Anyway, I appear at the beginning of the picture and if you blink an eye you might miss me, but it was marvelous to see how movies are made and to meet Mr. Gable. He was a real pro, and one of the nicest men."

Was she pleased with her performance? Mrs. Tree laughed. "I can't say that I was, not really."

As it happened, later that afternoon there was a special showing of a film in the United Nations Children's School. The school's director complained to Mrs. Tree that he looked as if he had a stiff neck in the movie. "Do I really hold my head like that when I talk?" he pleaded. "Never mind," she said, with the air of a professional. "It's always dreadful to see yourself on film."

Mrs. Tree has been photographed a great deal and so she must be used to the camera image of herself—she is often described as "patrician" or "classic."

She went on: "My daughters have an innate sense of how to dress. It's part of this new awareness. At sixteen I wasn't at all aware of what was becoming to me. I don't know why I distrusted my own judgment then. I'm quite sure I felt that my parents disapproved of me. I can't remember why I felt that way, which is interesting in itself. From the time I was eleven until just before my sixteenth year I felt it most strongly. I know that having four younger brothers had something to do with it—the feelings of competition, of course. Then, too, I imagine I felt that boys were more important, more valued than girls.

"I should say right away that the men in my family, my father and my grandfathers, felt that women were *very* important. What they thought, what they did, these things were never ignored. In fact, my father used to ask me frequently what I was going to do when I grew up. This question made me uncomfortable since I didn't have the slightest idea of what I wanted to do, besides go to a number of football games and parties and be popular and gay. And yet my father made it very clear that my thoughts and aspirations mattered to him. If I felt boys were more valued than girls, that thought came entirely from within me. It was something I felt in spite of all evidence to the contrary. Perhaps I needed to.

"I realize now how important it is to have encouragement from one's father. Recently I was at a seminar at Southern Methodist University in Texas, and so many of the girls there were discouraged because they had no feeling that their fathers cared about their careers or their work in the community. Some even said they had had difficulty in getting away to college at all. It was considered unfeminine or just useless to send a girl to college. It's a terrible handicap, to feel that your merit as a human being is limited because you happen to be female.

"I was always encouraged to think for myself, to become educated in the truest sense of the word. In fact, my father insisted that I go to college, against my will. When I was eighteen I was so vague, so feckless, I had no ideas beyond the immediate present. It wasn't the custom for the girls I knew to go to college, and I didn't want to go, either. He practically dragged me off physically, and I remember thinking he was absolutely brutal, that he didn't understand me at all if he could force me to do something like that. My mother was in favor of it too, but it was my father who really *made* me go. If he hadn't been so 'brutal,' I probably could have got out of it.

"It wasn't until college that I discovered the life of the mind, and it opened up new worlds for me. Very simply, I learned to think about ideas, to explore them. I had had a thoroughly good training in learning how to conjugate Latin verbs and memorize dates in ancient history, that sort of thing, but I had never opened my mind to new concepts. I had never thought about abstract problems or philosophical ideas, never grappled with them as I learned to do later. It was, literally, a whole new mental life. I felt it in my first college philosophy classes, and then I began to really read voraciously. I began to have a sense of myself as a person who could fit into the scheme of things around me. There wasn't so much time for parties and dances and just unadulterated fun, but I enjoyed myself much more. It gave me a new confidence.

"I began to see that my so-called confidence before had not been real. It wasn't confidence in myself or what I was, but just pride of position." She laughed. "Confidence in the position of Brownie captain, for example. It's possible to hold an office and feel confident in *it* without feeling confidence in yourself.

"In college I met other people who were interested in ideas and books, people who might tend to look down on my frivolity. I met people of all ages and kinds, but with one thing in common: they wanted to learn. Most of the men I knew were in law school then, and the people I saw were altogether more intelligent than I was and had different norms and standards to which I aspired. I'll never stop being grateful to my father for forcing me to go to college. It changed my life."

I looked up at the numerous framed diplomas in Mrs. Tree's office, honorary degrees, including Doctor of Laws (University of Pennsylvania) and Doctor of Humane Letters (Russell Sage College), and couldn't help but wonder if Mrs. Tree wasn't underestimating herself as she had been at sixteen. Is it possible to accomplish so much in later life if one isn't basically serious at sixteen?

"It's true that I was interested in politics at a very early age," she admitted. "But that was because it was dinner-table conversation in our family. Many men in my family were actively involved in politics, and I found the table talk fascinating. I understood very well my grandfather's principles in founding Groton. He wanted to instill in young men a sense of responsibility, to let them know they were taking part in their time. In fact, the motto of the school is 'service.' Many of the boys who attended Groton went on to public life, and they still do. I know that this had a great effect on me. In the midst of my frivolity I could still appreciate my grandfather's aspirations for the generation of young men growing up at that time. I can marvel now that with such excellent influences around me I remained so shallow.

"For a time in college I had my heart set on entering the diplomatic service. In fact I had taken all the necessary prerequisites when I was told by an ex-ambassador that President Roosevelt didn't accept women. 'If you're attractive they assume you'll marry a foreign diplomat before the year is out, and if you're not they feel you don't have what it takes to be successful.' That's the way he put it. How crushing to be denied something simply because you happen to be a woman. Now, in this day and age, things are much different. My older daughter, Frances, is a correspondent in Vietnam.

"I am so pleased with my children. My younger daughter, Penelope, went away to school for two years and didn't like it at all. She did her best, but she's back home now finishing out her last year of high school here, and she's much happier. I keep saying this, but it's so true: girls today have such a well-developed sense of self, of who they are. I am so impressed by my daughters' contemporaries. They seem to be passing through the teenage years with so much less pain than I did.

"Here's something I'd like to discuss with my daughters: What has caused this new generation of self-assured, delightful girls? They read more books than I did. They can discuss with a great deal of interest and knowledge everything from philosophy to the latest film. They are busy without being erratic. They think, really think, about things with depth and intelligence. They're really *very* good company. They seem able to be affectionate and easy with their parents, to communicate with the adult world in general. Perhaps most important of all, they are able to commit themselves to causes and ideas. At their age, I didn't look beyond myself. I was so far from being able even to accept myself as a worthwhile and important person. I don't think I was able to communicate with my parents very well, which was more my fault than theirs.

"What can have changed so much, made them so confident and inquiring? They don't even seem to go through awkward physical stages, as my generation did. I think a part of it is the pressure at school. There is such competition to get into schools now, it forces them to focus more sharply and develop faster. In a way, they have been forced to grow up faster, and yet it hasn't seemed to harm them. On the contrary.

"The tendency to involve themselves in causes—how remarkable! It seems extraordinary, unbelievable in fact, but I never really met a Negro until I was twenty-six. My daughters, of course, have traveled and met people of varying backgrounds and all colors from the time they were very small, and it has made them richer, fuller human beings. They never think in terms of color or race. What people don't realize in regard to the whole question of integration of schools is that the whites are short-changed as much as Negroes when they remain segregated. We miss so much when we're confined within such limiting circumstances. The rest of the community suffers just as much by permitting a segregated society to exist, only they don't realize it. The single most valuable thing which can happen to anyone, sixteen or ninety, is to meet people entirely different from oneself. It's the best way to broaden oneself and learn about the world in general. It makes life infinitely more rich and wonderful.

"Some people never stop being involved in life. They're the lucky ones. It's what I would wish for myself and my daughters. My parents are still tremendously active and involved and in the mainstream of things. My father was a bishop in the Episcopal Church, and when he retired he continued to function in the church as a curate, which is the lowest rung on the clerical ladder. He is still in contact with the people he served for so many years, and the good he is able to do in this rather humble capacity is a double-edged thing. It brings him great pleasure too. He never stops giving of himself and thus he never stops reaping the rewards of a lifetime of service. He and my mother are enormously involved in so many things, the ecumenical concept of bringing all the Protestant churches together, for one. And of course, civil rights. My mother has worked tirelessly for civil rights."

Mrs. Peabody has not only worked for civil rights; she has

gone to jail for her beliefs. About two years ago, the white-haired, seventy-five-year-old lady, wife of the retired Episcopal Bishop of Central New York and mother of the then Governor of Massachusetts, Endicott Peabody, was arrested for participating in civil rights demonstrations in St. Augustine, Florida. Mrs. Tree's daughter, Frances, wrote an article about her grandmother: "My Grandmother Is a Jailbird," which appeared in *The Reader's Digest* and helped launch a successful writing career.

"She's a very good writer," said her mother. "She's written for the Sunday *Times, The Atlantic Monthly, The Village Voice*, the London *Telegraph* and *Vogue*. Through *The Herald Tribune* she got accredited in Vietnam."

I was a little puzzled about what Mrs. Tree actually did at the United Nations. I knew she had served on a number of committees and delegations, and that she had been Ambassador to the United Nations Mission, but what was her current title?

"I'm the Personal Representative of the Secretary-General to the U.N. International School," she explained, and then with a smile: "It's mostly a fund-raising job. I get here at 9:30 just like everyone else, and I spend most of my day speaking to various foundations about donations for our projects. [The school exists for the children of delegates and members of the United Nations. Children from all over the world study together, bringing something of their own culture into each classroom and study period.] I'm going down to see a movie on the school now. I work very closely with the headmaster, and he and I will try to select some film clips to be shown on Channel 13 television."

And after this she left, walking with long, purposeful strides through the U.N. corridors and looking more like a fashion model than a woman with many responsibilities on her shoulders. I remembered something she had said earlier in the afternoon. "My family doesn't seem to be particularly artistic. I doubt very much that any of us could sit down and write a symphony or paint a great work of art. I certainly couldn't. But we *do* things, and perhaps that's what keeps the world going."

Suzanne Farrell

*At twenty-one, Suzanne Farrell is the youngest principal
dancer in the New York City Ballet. Critics and crowds first
took note of her when she was sixteen on a tour of Europe and
Russia with the company. The following year American audiences responded enthusiastically to her performance in* Movements for Piano and Orchestra. *And in the spring of 1965, she
won praise as Dulcinea in* Don Quixote, *a role created for
her by George Balanchine, choreographer of the New York City
Ballet.*

She was born Roberta Sue Ficker, on August 16, 1945, into a talented family. When, at eight years old, she began ballet lessons at the Cincinnati Conservatory, it was "because I was such a tomboy, my mother said she had to find something to keep me off the streets." It worked, and Miss Farrell became absorbed in the dance. As a girl, she daydreamed not about movie stars but about the New York City Ballet, Jacques d'Amboise and Balanchine.

In 1960 a Ford Foundation grant opened several scholarships to the School of American Ballet, a training school for the New York City Ballet. Ballerina Diana Adams found Suzanne Farrell on a country-wide talent search for the grant. On her fifteenth birthday, she auditioned for Mr. Balanchine and was accepted.

She moved with her family to New York, and set to work with ardor. When not at school, she spent hours at the New York City Ballet, studying the dancers. About this time, she adopted her stage name, Suzanne Farrell.

A year later, she was taken into the corps de ballet. *At sixteen, she was the youngest member of the company, and within another year, she had danced her first solo role, in* La Valse. *It was followed by a more important role in* Serenade.

When she was eighteen, her fairy-tale dreams came true. She replaced the ailing Diana Adams in a leading role one week before the opening of Movements for Piano and Orchestra. *In the ballet, she literally danced into the arms of her childhood idol, Jacques d'Amboise. Later, in two benefit performances of the new ballet,* Don Quixote, *she had the unique experience of dancing with George Balanchine himself. It was the master's first performance in twenty years.*

Suzanne has been called "a jewel of a girl, shy, sweet, responsive." When she dances, her style is youthful, energetic, and seems effortlessly graceful.

Suzanne Farrell

M̲r̲. B̲a̲l̲a̲n̲c̲h̲i̲n̲e̲ likes to describe me as a cat, because I'm swift," said Suzanne Farrell. She seemed to prefer his natural metaphor to the more matter-of-fact description of herself as principal dancer, an accomplishment about which she is remarkably modest. A smooth-skinned, never-quite-still girl with large eyes (Mr. Balanchine has also been quoted as saying "her soul is in her eyes"), she has long brown hair that falls to mid-back. Sometimes she wears her hair up, but either way she looks younger than her twenty-one years.

As she spoke, sitting in a side room resembling a small gymnasium at the New York State Theater, the air conditioner hummed against her voice. A price tag still attached to it made irritable cricks. The walls of the room were porous beige concrete, and Miss Farrell and I faced each other across a bare, schoolmarmish desk. Even in such a setting she was poised, moving and talking with a shy but strong self-possession.

"I haven't really changed much, I'm pretty much the same as

I was at sixteen," she said. "I used to love to skate and swim and I still do, though I can't skate any more because I have to be careful of my ankles. But I still swim like a fish. That year was my first season in New York, only it was at City Center. Then the following summer, when I was still sixteen, I joined the New York City Ballet. I had already danced my first public performance back in Cincinnati when I was younger. It was at the Opera when I was thirteen; I lied about my age because you were supposed to be at least fourteen, but by the time they found out, it was all right. I was fourteen and I was dancing.

"When I first came to New York, I was going to school, Professional Children's School. I would get up around eight and inevitably I would be late to school—always, no matter how hard I tried, I just couldn't get there. Maybe five minutes late, but I just couldn't get there before the bell went off. It was a private school, and I would have class from 9:30 until ten o'clock. English. Then I would leave quietly, while the class was still going on, and hurry up and go out for a 10:30 ballet class.

"Ballet classes and academic classes were in two different schools. The two have nothing to do with each other except that the academic school has an understanding that the students may leave because this is their lifework. The school is geared to the child's career. After ballet, I would make it back to school in time for lunch. Which I didn't need. I spent so little time in school as it was, because of my ballet, that it was sort of unfortunate that when I finally could be in school, it was lunchtime when nothing was going on. Then, after that, maybe an hour and a half more of class study, and then I would have to leave again for a toe class from 2:30 until four. Afterwards I'd walk home through the city sometimes, if the weather was nice, and look in the stores, because I didn't live too far from the ballet school. And then sort of collapse. Not really collapse, but get something to eat and begin on school-work.

"At night that year I used to go watch the performances of the ballet company—that was before I myself had gotten in, when I was still with City Center. It was very inspiring. I admired them all because they're all really wonderful dancers, but particularly Diana Adams because she's tall and I just love the way she moves. She was the one who chose me in Cincin-nati to come and audition for Mr. Balanchine for a Ford Foundation scholarship.

"Later, she helped me a little on my hands, which were awful. I just didn't hold my hands right. It's very complicated, but when you're at class, Mr. Balanchine wants you to hold your hands a particular way because it provides tension—no, not tension, but strength in the rest of your body. You must bend your wrist and cup your palm. I remember lots of times I used to have a ball, a small rubber ball, you know, to get the feeling of a hollow in my hand. I'd dance with this rubber ball—just at the bar, I'd take class with it. Of course, that didn't mean that onstage I had to look like I had a ball in my hand.

"When I first joined the company, I was so excited at just being there and trying to dance well and make Mr. Balanchine notice me and help me that I never thought too much about roles, you know, star roles. Sometimes he would make me so nervous. He'd talk to me or correct me in class and I'd look at him and say to myself, 'Oh, my goodness, he's correcting me, he's correcting me, this wonderful person is correcting me.' I would be so flabbergasted that I wouldn't hear what he was correcting me *on*. Then he would say, 'Do you understand?' and I'd just sort of nod my head, 'Yes, I understand.' And he would walk away. But I wouldn't know what he'd said, I was so in awe of him.

"Actually, it seems he didn't even know I was around until ten months after I'd been in the company. Then one of the ballerinas became ill and couldn't dance. I was just standing there, watching rehearsal, and everyone was upset because no one knew her part. Mr. Balanchine looked over at me and said, 'Let Suzanne do it, she doesn't have anything else to do.' Which was sort of funny.

"So I had to learn a ballet called *Serenade* in two days. It was very, very fast, and I was very nervous about it. I worked on it and as far as I was concerned, I wasn't going to swim any more until after this big performance—no more swimming, which I love to do. There was no time and I was busy thinking about the role. I remembered that Diana had said to me once, 'You should know a role backwards and forwards and inside out so well that when you go onstage, you don't have to think about it. Your body does the thinking.' And it's really true. If dancing is going to be so much of a chore, then you shouldn't do it, because you should enjoy what you're doing. So I thought of that, and I would do this particular role five times every night before I went to bed.

"I still have that approach to dancing. I enjoy it, except there are one or two ballets that absolutely petrify me. One is *Ballet Imperial*, which is very, very difficult and fast. It was hard for me at first and it's still hard, but not as hard. Only two of us do it at present, Patricia McBride, my dressing-room-mate and myself, and we both sort of feel not so good at it.

"I was extremely nervous and excited when I made my debut with the company. I had collected pictures and sent away for pictures and had a huge scrapbook and read a lot and lived in the library. I knew a lot about the New York City Ballet. And I prayed, but of course I had never dreamed that I would be in the company. Finally, when I did get in, I never dreamed that I would be a principal dancer. I didn't dare ask for more than just being here. So here I am. Sometimes I still look in the mirror and say: 'Do you know who you are?' Not that I'm anybody, but you know I don't look much different than I did when I was younger, and I still feel the same. Now, actually, I'm more mature and I've had more experience. I'm more responsible, but I'm still basically the same person I was then. I still work just as hard.

"Occasionally now I go to visit my friends from dancing school in Cincinnati. They're all either still going to school or married and have children. Not that there's anything wrong with that, it's just that they're still there, and now I've been all over the world. You know, until I got into the company, I'd never been in an airplane before, and now I've been in Russian airplanes—and it's really quite a switch."

Miss Farrell's first ride in a Russian airplane was at sixteen, when she traveled with the New York City Ballet to Moscow on a goodwill mission.

"In every city we went to in Russia, they organized a tour for us. They treated us very nicely, and they were often curious about us, about our clothing and our shoes, for example. I think they had never smoked American cigarettes, either, because when we were in the buses, little kids and other people would say, 'Cigarette, cigarette?' They'd want us to give them a cigarette or chewing gum, and in return they'd give us a pin that said 'Russia' or else an emblem of theirs. They had heard about our cigarettes and chewing gum, and they wanted to try them.

"The people were nice and the children were very cute—fat little cheeks and cold and all bundled up. And our audiences were wonderful. They were really impressed with what we were doing and thought it was fascinating that we had advanced so, as far as ballet is concerned. We weren't still doing the ballets that we had twenty years ago. We *can* do those ballets, but we also do more up-to-date things. We've evolved into something else, whereas they still do only the old classics. It really would be sort of unrewarding, I should think, for a ballerina to do only *Swan Lake* or only *Giselle.* I know I wouldn't like to do that. They're nice ballets, but we have better ballets. It's nice to do a modern work, then a jazzy one, and then a very classical one, and then maybe an acting one. I wouldn't be a bit surprised if the Russians aren't taking a lot of our ballets to learn how we do the more modern works."

In New York, Miss Farrell and her sister, who is a pianist ("She is very talented—she knows more about dancing than I do about music."), share an apartment with their mother on the upper West Side of Manhattan.

"My mother says that I was a terrible, terrible brat when I was younger. I kept denying it, and the more I denied it, the guiltier I was. So now I can say, 'Yes, you're right, I was a terrible brat when I was younger.' And from movies that we have—we just got out the old movies and we were looking at them over Christmas—I guess I was really terribly bratty, spoiled. I always had to have my own way. But for some reason when I came to New York and I saw how many girls there were trying to study and how good they were and how many better ones there were, I really started to work and tried not to be so spoiled. I tried to be more understanding, and I think I have developed that over the years.

"Now my mother is very proud of me, and she trusts me and knows that I must be responsible and intelligent, otherwise I wouldn't have . . . I couldn't be trusted with the things that I do. She is a nurse, which keeps her away from eight in the morning until eight at night. So we get along very well, probably because we're not with each other constantly. And it's only normal that when my mother works with her patient all day long, she'll want to be alone some of the time. Or maybe she'll want to be with my sister and me, play cards or whatever. When we start back to regular performances next Tuesday, I'll be dancing every night, so my mother will probably come to a lot of the ballets then. Afterwards we go home and get a little snack and perhaps all sit in the bedroom and talk, because that's where the television is and the two beds and the Hi-Fi.

"I like to cook, so I usually cook for my sister. If I can't eat it, I like to watch her eat it. Weight doesn't matter with her, and I like to have cake or something in the house and make coffee and serve things. I like to be around food. Probably if I ate I wouldn't get fat, but I usually don't eat much all day long, maybe toasted bagels or an English muffin in the morning, and then maybe shrimp cocktail in the afternoon, or maybe nothing but coffee, a piece of cheese or an egg. It's just that I'd rather eat after the performance when I can enjoy it and know that I don't have to get into a costume.

"It's funny, even when I get a chance to get away, sometimes I'd rather be here at the theater, I'm so wrapped up in dancing. Recently I went to visit my other sister who just had a baby in November—I'm an aunt twice now. It was for three days just before Christmas. I knew that *Nutcracker* was going on down here, and I wasn't needed because it wasn't my set. There were forty-one performances and we had divided them up. I wasn't scheduled to dance until a couple of weeks later. But still, I'm so used to being here, or at least in the city or where the company is, and it was such a funny feeling for me—it's only an hour by plane, but it seemed so far away from my usual routine. I began to feel very ill at ease. I had fun with my nephew, and it was nice for a little rest and a diversion, but when it's so out of the ordinary, I felt, you know, 'Oh, I've got to get back. I'm getting out of shape. I've got to take classes.'

"Ballet has always been uppermost. At sixteen, there were some parties, and I used to like to play kickball and baseball. But they were only secondary. It was mostly just one track, ballet. I was never at school very long, so I didn't know many boys or girls. The girls and boys I did know were in ballet, and they were just as busy as I was. And tired. Parties weren't so important, because when you had danced all day you didn't feel like dancing at night.

"Even now I don't like to go to, say, discotheques. You will never find me in one. I don't like them. I don't like crowds, unorganized people, and they're rude because they bump into you when they're dancing. And you don't even need a partner, you can just get up there. In ballet, you don't always have a partner, either, but you do, for example, in a *pas de deux*. And it's more lovely to look at than the modern dances now. They have no elegance to them. I love to waltz. Why don't people waltz any more? I don't mean I'm old-fashioned, not by any means, but I don't like these mod fashions—cutaway dresses and crazy colors."

She was wearing a dress that was almost shocking pink. "Isn't that a crazy color?" I asked.

"It's not." She laughed. "You can be up to date but you don't have to be crazy with your clothes. I don't like the real, real short dresses and I don't like the crazy colors, all different colors mixed together. And I don't like dresses that are cut away at the waist or in the arms. Dancers look good in almost any style clothing because they have nice figures and they know how to carry themselves. Lots of girls that I went to ballet school with when I was very, very young haven't danced in five years or so, but they're all glad they had it. It gave them poise and grace.

"As far as clothes go, I don't like to stick to a fashion or a vogue. Everyone has their own taste, and I think I feel secure about mine. I'm happier not looking like every other girl in the street. Not that I'm perfect. When I first joined the company at sixteen, I used to be terribly, terribly bad at makeup. No one ever told me how to make up. I didn't know why you put brown stuff here and blue stuff there, or blue stuff here and brown stuff there. I didn't know why you would draw a line a certain way. I only copied other people, you know. If I saw somebody I liked, I would copy. I knew you emphasized your eyebrows and things like that, but I didn't really know any of the particulars of makeup. And I was very, very bad. I'm extremely bad at eyebrows. I could get the right one on, but I couldn't reverse my arm and get the left one on. It would take me two hours just to do my makeup. Once I put my left eyebrow on thirteen times, put it on and took it off, because it wasn't right. It was too arched, or it wasn't arched enough, or it was frayed. Probably the majority of people, unless they have glasses on, wouldn't have seen that one eyebrow was more curved than the other, but I saw it and it made me feel ugly, so I would take it off.

"In my free time, I like to shop. I like to buy clothes, dresses and shoes. I like to buy for our apartment and for my nephews because they have such cute things for kids. Or sometimes I'll meet my girlfriend in the company or be with my sister or my mother, and sometimes I just like to be alone. When I have time that isn't devoted to dancing, I don't like to be tied down to anything in particular, I like to be able to do just what I want to do or what strikes my fancy at the moment. A dancer's life is usually so regimented that when you have a few hours to yourself, you don't like to have to, say, go to the dentist because you haven't been there in a long time and this is the only chance you're going to get until the next layoff.

"During the day, I usually think about what I have to do at night. I would never think of going to a movie in the afternoon if I had to dance at night. I remember I did that once when I was younger. And I was so relaxed by the time of the perform-ance that I wasn't quite ready. I mean I was ready, I got there in plenty of time, and I did my bar, and I did everything as usual, but I had been so sort of normal during the day that I wasn't in a completely ballet mood at night. I wasn't sloppy or unprepared, but it's just so different and so unsafe to go to a movie in the afternoon and then still expect to be, you know, change yourself into someone else to perform for an audience at night. So I'll never do that again. I'll save all my movies for my free days.

"I think, when you're in ballet, your training is so intense and you have to give up so much outside activity that you become more mature and responsible at an earlier age. Girls my age now will probably be in college. Of course, college can be a wonderful experience, but I think that some girls who go to college don't get as much out of it as they should. I guess they think: 'If I go to college I might meet a nice man and get married.' But that isn't why a person should go to college. Perhaps some of them aren't really aware of what they want out of life. I'm very fortunate. I know that I have to dance to be happy, and if I'm not dancing, I'm very unhappy.

"On the other hand, a dancer's career doesn't always last so long. If you're unfortunate, you have an injury. Then you are suspended for a while. For example, I have a bad knee. I decided to have it operated on in May and see if they think I may have a tumor. So now I'm just going to dance for all I'm worth until May. I'll probably have to forfeit my summer as far as dancing is concerned, but I think that's the time to do it. Anyway, most dancers' careers end around forty or so, which is very, very young for a woman, you know, very young. But I could always teach, and, oh yes, eventually marry, though marriage doesn't seem to have mixed very well with dancing in the past. I'd like to get married eventually, though, when the right man and the right time comes.

"But now," she added, "I like the discipline. I need to be channeled. I'm healthy and I can take the work. Of course everyone goes through periods of depression. I used to think, and sometimes I still do, why do I go to class every morning and try to turn out my feet and try to perfect all my steps when the average person in the audience doesn't know that I'm technically correct? Why do I struggle to get better when they appreciate what you give them anyway? But it's sort of an unexplainable something inside of you. I guess it's my heart and my soul. I feel that if this is what I'm going to do and this is what I like to do, then I have to do the best I can. Whether the people in the audience appreciate it or know it or not, it doesn't matter. Because I'm not only dancing for them, I'm dancing for myself and Mr. Balanchine and for the welfare of the company.

"Besides, it's not all work. I may be a principal dancer by the standards of the company, but I can still be a human being. When I get home, and even sometimes in class, I can be sort of silly. If I'm a ballerina onstage, I'm just a regular girl offstage. I don't think there's anything wrong with that. Just because people know me because of my work doesn't mean that I'm any better than somebody who is a plumber or a secretary. We're all the same people.

"What is important to me aside from dancing? To be honest and sincere, I think. The people in this company fortunately are all very nice, and I would like to think that everybody in the world is nice and no one speaks ill of anyone; and everybody that says 'you're a nice person' sincerely believes it. But unfortunately everyone does not. Mr. Balanchine is a wonderful person and the people connected with the company are too. I think I'm very lucky to be doing what I wanted to do with wonderful people because, especially in New York, you can so easily get into the wrong hands or start to think, you know, competitively. You shouldn't be competitive and you shouldn't be envious. Even if I hadn't become a principal dancer, I would be so glad that I was in the company that I wouldn't be envious if someone else were a ballerina.

"You meet so few sincere people. I can't imagine when someone tells me something, that it's not true. I believe it because I try to always tell the truth. The saying, 'If you can't say anything nice, don't say anything at all'—well, that's a nice saying but it doesn't necessarily always apply. If I see someone dance and I don't like their dancing, that doesn't mean they're a bad dancer. Because they may do something very, very nicely which I admire, but then they may not be what I want to fashion myself after. So you can say, 'Oh, you have lovely arms.' You don't have to say, 'Oh, you aren't a very good dancer.' I always try to be sincere. Mr. Balanchine is sincere and honest, and if a person as wonderful and intelligent—the genius that he is—can be humble and human, then certainly I can try to be humble and human because I am nobody compared to him. So I really look for sincerity in people more so than, well, 'Are you famous?' 'How much do you know?' 'What's your IQ?'

"These things you live with. Long after my career is over, when I finish dancing, I'm still going to be a person. I was a person before I was a dancer, and so it's up to me to keep it that way."

Sandra Hochman

"Sandra Hochman . . . has an instinctive rapport with language. She doesn't strive to impose metaphor on experience; metaphor and myth simply befall her." So Denise Levertov *described Miss Hochman's talent in a review of her first book of poetry,* Manhattan Pastures, *published in 1963 in the* Yale Young Poets *series. A second volume of poetry,* The Vaudeville Marriage, *was published recently. She has contributed an essay to a Lincoln Center book,* Theatre, Volume I, *and is now writing more poems and prose. Her poems have appeared in* The New Yorker, The Nation, Poetry, Partisan Review *and other magazines.*

Born in Manhattan, September 11, 1936, Sandra grew up mostly in the country. She attended a private high school, Cherry Lawn, and graduated from one of this country's most liberal colleges, Bennington. She is married to Harvey Leve, an international lawyer.

Shortly after college, she acted in the off-Broadway production of The Iceman Cometh *in the Circle in the Square Theater. She then went to Paris to live and study for three years.*

In 1965–66, she was poet-in-residence at Fordham University, and has since become something of a "traveling poet" as well, giving readings at Sarah Lawrence, Cornell, Yale, Bennington and other universities. For a while Miss Hochman conducted an interview and reading program, Poems in Print, *on radio station WBAI. This gave her the opportunity, she says, "to interview almost every living poet in this country." Recently she and poet Muriel Rukeyser were the subjects of a television report,* The Woman, the Poet, the City.

Sandra Hochman

Oᴜᴛsɪᴅᴇ, an icy, wind-driven rain was spattering down. Sandra Hochman had lit a fire in anticipation of my arrival, and we sat close to it in a corner of her living room sipping vodka from tiny blue-and-white seventeenth-century Japanese teacups. A symphony was playing on the hi-fi. My soaking raincoat (I had forgotten my umbrella) had been taken away. The fire smelled of autumn and danced orange, a small sun working against the gray day. "This is very nice," I said, and Miss Hochman's eyes smiled an instant before the rest of her face. "Vodka is good for taking away a chill," she said.

Sandra Hochman's eyes are quite green, her hair is blond, her smile is warm and friendly. She could be the girl next door, only grown up and married and poised. In neither dress nor manner is she the wild-haired bohemian poet who hears secret music piped on some private wavelength. She wore a modish pink Thai silk coat over white slacks. On her left hand, next to a wedding band, was a beautiful jade, pearl and diamond ring which she said she had designed herself.

Her apartment, in a converted town house off Fifth Avenue, is feminine and pleasant. The living room is large and light, fronted by many windows overlooking the street and, obliquely, Central Park. Books cover two walls from floor to ceiling. In a far corner there is a tan, often-used Steinway piano. Couches and chairs in restful hues of maroon and light pink, many paintings on the walls, a light-colored oriental rug in the center of the room, contrasting with darker polished-wood floors—the total feeling is one of calm and civilized comfort.

Calmly, too, Miss Hochman began: "Sixteen was a year of changes—first, graduation from boarding school, then working in a camp as a teacher, and then entering college. I was changing very much too. I was the youngest girl in my graduating class and the youngest freshman at Bennington. At sixteen I was very aware of my age and I was proud of always being the youngest.

"Physically, I was chubbier, I think, but the same height as I am now. I was friendly, trusting anything or anyone, studious, a dreamer, a bookworm, had a terrible singing voice but I loved to sing, loved dancing, horses, causes, boys, cheerleading, Christmas pageants and words. I devoured everything printed: plays, history, any kind of book. I never found a book that I didn't enjoy. But I don't think I was an ordinary student. That's because the school I grew up in, Cherry Lawn in Darien, Connecticut, was an extraordinary school. There is nothing typical about an education at a progressive boarding school. The teachers were excellent. I can remember reading T. S. Eliot and James Joyce in the sixth grade. The school emphasized outdoor living and all of the arts and history. My eyes were opened to history, modern European history and ancient history, and poetry, as things that were alive, not just subjects in textbooks. By the time I graduated, I was quite well read in contemporary literature and owned a Dylan Thomas record, which I loved and listened to the way people listen to Bob Dylan today. I also remember that my favorite work of fiction was Thornton Wilder's *The Bridge of San Luis Rey,* and the poem I read most frequently was T. S. Eliot's 'The Wasteland.'

"On graduation day I delivered the speech given by the student who had been at Cherry Lawn longest. I had been there for nine years, and I had the feeling that sixteen was my year of liberty. Graduation was freedom.

"Well, here I am talking about life at sixteen, but I should also talk about inner life, what went on inside. I had a pretty wild imagination and I was also a dreamer. Quite frightened about some things, such as 'being alone,' and yet always enthusiastic, a trouble-maker, and what I suppose must be called an idealist. I sometimes thought of being an actress, or a dancer, or a writer, or a crusader for people's rights. I was a jumble of dreams.

"One of the disappointments of my sixteenth year was not being accepted at the college that I dreamed of going to, Sarah Lawrence. I think I answered the questions on the long application form in a rather simple-minded fashion and constantly misspelled the name of the college. But it was a blow not to be accepted. Then I visited Bennington College in Vermont and immediately felt at home there. I loved the Vermont countryside, the simple white houses, the teachers I met and the atmosphere of vitality I felt there. I was overjoyed when I was accepted at Bennington and have never regretted this marvelous experience. At Bennington, thanks to some of my professors, who were my heroes as well as teachers, I developed an interest in writing.

"The summer when I was sixteen I was an assistant to a

drama teacher, Maurice Edwards, at a music camp called Beaupré in Lenox, Massachusetts. I was enamored of music and theater—I still am—and got that job so I could be near Tanglewood and the music festival. I loved teaching that summer, and, of course, I was exhilarated by the anticipation of college."

Suddenly Miss Hochman laughed in a girlish way. "Oh yes," she said, "I was an intellectual snob as far as boys were concerned. I was only interested in boys I could learn something from. I remember that all of the boys I liked being with that summer were musicians at Tanglewood. I had one friend who was a young conductor from Mexico, and I admired him for being completely involved with his music. At boarding school nobody had dates. You were just together in school and you weren't frightened by talking with boys, and you didn't act any differently with them than you would with your own girlfriends. At boarding school you went to classes and took part in activities with boys in a very natural way. I think this made it easier for me to think of having boys as really good friends.

"I remember my sixteenth summer. The person I admired most was Leonard Bernstein, who was then *the* brilliant young conductor at Tanglewood. I had picture postcards of him, bought in Hagard's drugstore, tacked to my wall. Although I had arranged to be introduced to him at least five times, I wanted very badly to *talk* to him, and I got the brilliant idea of interviewing him for an imaginary newspaper called the *Beaupré News*. I convinced a counselor who was much older than I (she was a sophomore in college) to act as my secretary. We made a collection from all our friends to raise enough money for the taxi that would take us to Blantyre where he was living. Mr. Bernstein was very nice. I'm sure he knew that we were young kids who just had a crush on him. Although he had turned down lots of interviews, he was kind enough to see us. While I was interviewing him he was interrupted by a phone call from *Time* magazine (whose circulation, needless to say, was larger than ours). Of course I knew the answers to all the questions I asked him since I had made a detailed study of his life, but I remember one thing he said that influenced me. He mentioned during this interview that when he had studied at Harvard, he had majored in the things he knew the least about rather than majoring in music. I remembered this later when I was at Bennington, and consequently took a lot of courses in subjects that I was interested in but of which I had no knowledge. Leonard Bernstein was in a way a symbolic person. To me, he represented intelligence and attractiveness, energy, all of which I admired very much. Also he was *versatile*, a talent I still greatly respect. For example, what is more marvelous than the works of history, novels and poetry, written by that genius, Robert Graves?

"At sixteen my closest friend was probably my boarding-school English teacher, a dedicated man who was always encouraging and kind to me. His name is Basil Burwell—we called him Bazz—and he still teaches English and theater at Cherry Lawn as well as finding time to write novels and to direct plays off-Broadway. He was the person who first taught me to read poetry. He was a good friend to all the students. We could go and talk to him about our lives, our dreams and other important matters. Aside from Bazz, I had only one or two close friends, and the people I liked being with best were creative and imaginative. I had an affinity for people with talent or a sense of humor, or both. All of this admiration ties in with my values at the time. What was important to me then, as now, was what a person was doing to add something to the world.

"About college: when I got to Bennington and started studying I was overwhelmed by my ignorance and began charging ahead with all sorts of new discoveries. I read the works of Fraser, Joyce, Yeats for the first time. Very exciting. I felt free to grow and learn in the atmosphere of Bennington. I liked the idea of writing end-of-term papers and also the informality that comes when there are no marks.

"When I remember myself at sixteen, I remember a girl who trusted—everyone and everything. Although I was born in New York City, I think that I was naive because I hadn't grown up in a city environment. I was protected by schools. I had grown up in Connecticut and spent my summers either in camps or on my grandfather's farm in Goshen, New York, so I was a healthy outdoor girl, unsophisticated, troubled, I suppose, by a lot of things but still able to enjoy the sound of birds and the colors of plants and the shapes of shells. I had a love for plants and animals and a love for being in the fresh air. Even now I like to escape from New York as often as possible and be by the sea or in the country. I walk a lot in the city and try to spend as much time in the country as I can, in the tall grass of the country or by the ocean. I remember how unbelievably beautiful it was to experience that first autumn in Vermont. I was absolutely awed by the colors.

"At sixteen I wasn't very athletic, even though I used to steal as much time as I could from studying to walk around by myself on the grounds of Cherry Lawn. I didn't excel at sports, but I did spend a lot of free time down at the school stables. Riding was the one sport I enjoyed. I had a favorite horse called Ho-Hum. And, much to my joy and surprise, I was voted a cheerleader. But I was a failure at basketball and couldn't make the hockey team. I was quite relieved to find there weren't any sports at Bennington."

Miss Hochman paused. "Let's see," she said, "what else can I say about sixteen? I loved to laugh and I was attracted to funny people who could make me laugh. I was always telling jokes or listening to them, and constantly turning situations into satires which I would retell to my friends. I had an appetite for life, for food, for music, for seeing things and traveling.

"Speaking of traveling, the summer before sixteen I had talked my father into letting me go to Europe with an academic travel association. Believe it or not, I joined a study group of Catholic physical education teachers, many of them in their sixties, who came from Saint Louis. I had convinced my father that I would be *safe* traveling with them. It was really amusing because I wasn't at all interested in meeting other physical education teachers abroad, but it was the only way I could get to see Europe. I discovered that I felt at home in Europe. I couldn't wait to grow up and go back.

"One question that tormented me was 'What will I do with my life?' I was haunted by this question and I didn't have a good answer. I wasn't influenced by my family. My parents were divorced. My father had certain ideas about what he wanted me to do and be, but I was disobedient and did more or less what I wanted to do rather than what I was told. Often, I'm afraid, I disobeyed him. I felt that each person had their own life to live and I wasn't going to let anyone tell me what to do. There were so many alternatives. One day I was going to be a novelist, the next day I was considering living in an ashram [a religious retreat] in India. I was excited by all the possibilities of life, overcharged, I think.

"At sixteen I had fallen in love thousands of times, and out of love again. I wasn't serious about any one person; my heart hadn't been broken by anyone. Perhaps that's why I was relatively happy—I lived very much in the kingdom of my imagination. It was a time of innocence, naiveté and development."

"Did you think of yourself as a poet then?" I asked.

"Well, as a matter of fact, sixteen was the first year that I began to publish poetry, but I didn't think of myself as a poet then and I *still* don't think of myself as one. Howard Nemerov, one of my teachers at Bennington, once said to me, 'Remember, you're not really a poet until you're forty and still writing.' That meant very much to me and I think it's true. The word *poet* is an honor that I give to other people like Theodore Roethke, Wallace Stevens or Marianne Moore. By the way, she is one of the writers that I admire most. 'In Distrust of Merits' is one of my favorite poems. So, I think of myself as a person, not a poet, but I do think of myself as an *observant* person, and I want to put these observations in books that will delight people. Through writing I'd like to be able to create something that would be of importance to others, so they can say, 'Oh yes! She knows *that* too.' "

She paused again, remembering. "Everything was so different for me when I was sixteen. One difference is that I'm now beginning to discover how to be alone without being lonely. I remember from time to time suffering terribly from loneliness. Now I sometimes look forward to being alone, especially if I'm writing. I have a wonderful husband and I see him in the evening, so I don't always mind being alone during the day. When I was sixteen I wanted someone besides my parents and teachers to be close to, and I didn't have anyone."

"Did your loneliness have anything to do with your parents being divorced?" I asked.

Miss Hochman thought for a moment. "I don't know," she said. "Perhaps. I didn't really have a home then, at least that's the way it seemed to me. Now I do have one. Knowing that I can leave home and come back to it is a wonderful feeling. I used to think divorce was the worst thing, and I suppose I thought of it as being partly responsible for my loneliness. But now I think that being lonely is very much a part of life. I might have been lonely even if my parents hadn't been divorced. And now I've learned to make friends with this loneliness and use it. I feel that I'd like to do something to help children from divorced homes feel less alone and lonely. I think I touch on this problem in many of the poems in *The Vaudeville Marriage* and in other poems I've written.

"One way I ended my loneliness was through books. Loneliness drove me to reading. You can't be a writer unless you love to read. Reading has made me feel very close to so many writers I've never met, writers who are no longer alive: Pasternak and Lorca, Sean O'Casey, William Carlos Williams—the list is endless. These people seem as real to me as my own family. I also think that loneliness is really the other side of humor. Dark humor has always been part of my involvement with life. I never knew when to cry or when to laugh—and sometimes I do both at once.

"And, I still enjoy the same wild enthusiasms for writing, music, sculpture, philosophy that I did at sixteen. I'm always in some state of enthusiasm about the work of some artist that I'm discovering, or perhaps rediscovering. This year I've been listening, for example, to a lot of opera records and finding some operas that I never heard before. One of my fantasies is that someday someone will ask me to write the scenario or story for a new ballet. I'm still faithful to my love for music. Sometimes friends come over and play chamber music, which is one way of listening to miracles. Enthusiasm is so much a part of my life that I get worried if I have no enthusiasm for a day or two," Miss Hochman said. Then she smiled at her exaggeration.

"I still feel very ignorant," she went on earnestly, "and our house is always overflowing with books. Right now I'm starting to go deeper into my knowledge of Asia, to expand my reading about the cultures of the Far East. After my husband and I were married, we lived for a year in Hong Kong. We had a fabulous trip coming home through Southeast Asia, Cambodia, Thailand and the Middle East. That was wonderful; I learned so much. I think the future will see people sending their children abroad to study as well as just to college here. Through traveling you come alive to the bigness of the world; you realize the enormity of what there is to see and learn. I'd rather spend money on travel than on anything else. In fact, traveling for me is the only bargain there is in the world.

"I've always liked to travel. The first place I ever visited was Boston, a long way from Hong Kong! I remember I lost my passport once, when I was fifteen with the physical education teachers in Paris. I was praying that it would stay lost forever and that I would be forced to remain an exile in France for the rest of my life. Unfortunately it was found.

"On that first visit to Europe I was saddened and moved by the realization of how much people had suffered during the war. I wrote my first real poem, I think, about that suffering. Even now, I think that traveling spurs me on to a lot of insights and new poems. Very often, mental travel notes develop into poems. Right now I am working on some poems that incorporate observations from my life in Hong Kong. I've always written about places, as well as experiences and people.

"For me, everything does seem to come back to writing and reading. After I graduated from Bennington I worked in New York City in off-Broadway theater. I was in *The Iceman Cometh* in the Circle in the Square Theater. I missed my cue one night because I was reading *Gimpel the Fool* by Isaac Bashevis Singer; I was so involved in finishing the story that I almost forgot to go back onstage. I realized then that reading and writing were much more important to me than acting." She turned her thoughts to being sixteen again. "When I met someone new then, I could talk very easily if I felt comfortable; but if I felt uncomfortable, I couldn't even open my mouth. Some people thought I was very talkative; others, that I was terribly shy. It's the same way today. Well, I'm prone to daydreaming by myself. One of my favorite daydreams when I was sixteen was to decorate houses in my mind, and I still do that. I love antiques and I build houses in my mind and furnish them.

"As for differences between then and now—today I enjoy dressing up once in a while, but at sixteen I hated clothes. I usually went around in shirt and filthy dungarees, and dressed like a tomboy as often as possible. I was suspicious of clothes, in fact of all material things, and thought of them as something to avoid. They were dangerous to your soul. I suppose it was a fear of being corrupted, but more than that, I envied simplicity in people. I was attracted to the Quakers for that reason and had spent my sophomore summer of high school in a Quaker camp. I liked naturalness, not the artificiality of the bohemians and their exaggerated self-consciousness. And naturalness is still a thing I look for in people and in poems. I still dislike artificiality. Even at sixteen, I think I could detect easily what was artificial and phony."

The fire had died down by now, and we had long since finished our tiny drams of vodka. Miss Hochman's husband was taking her to see Norman Mailer's play, *The Deer Park,* that evening and she wanted to dress for the theater. I had one more question. "What advice," I asked, "do you think would have helped you most when you were sixteen?"

Her hand went to her chin and she pondered, looking at the clouds through the windows. Finally she said, "Well, I'm sure everyone did tell me very good things, but I didn't understand them then." She paused again. "I suppose the best advice would have been to believe more in myself. Of course, if they had told me that, I wouldn't really have known what they meant. Belief in myself has come only recently. If I had been more confident when I was sixteen, oh, it would have been much nicer."

Eileen Ford

Eileen Ford is vice-president of the Ford Agency, the world's most glamorous model agency, with a main office in New York and a branch in Paris (her husband is president of the firm). Twenty years ago, when the Fords started their business, model agencies were run in a haphazard, offhand manner. Frequently, a model was merely sent out on a job, and it was up to her to collect a fee and pay the agency. The Fords developed a new system which has now become standard in the business: they paid models immediately and collected their fees for them.

[68]

Another innovation of Mrs. Ford's was setting up introductory appointments between clients and new models who had successfully completed three months training with her agency. Mrs. Ford cares passionately about the agency and has a protective attitude toward "her girls." She is, as well, a personal friend to many of them.

She was born Eileen Otte in 1925, the only girl in a family of four children, and grew up in Great Neck on the North Shore of Long Island. She attended Great Neck's public schools and in 1942 enrolled at Barnard College in New York City, majoring in psychology. While still a student, in 1944 she married Gerard Ford. For a year after graduation she worked as a photographer's stylist, and then, in 1947, she and her husband opened their agency; she was then twenty-two.

The Fords now have four children: Jamie, who is twenty; Billy, fourteen; Katie, eleven; and Lacey, nine. The family has two homes, a townhouse in Manhattan's East Seventies and a summer place in Quogue, Long Island. They go abroad frequently, vacationing in Europe and Scandinavia.

Eileen Ford

Mrs. Ford was at the front desk of her modeling agency industriously taking Christmas presents out of a big cardboard carton. The presents were for "her girls." "They're really lovely presents," she said, brushing her mustang-brown hair back of one ear. "I hope there'll be one left over for me."

The phone rang often, and she took calls, checked gift cards, made notations, and looked up at me with alert interest, all at once. A brunette in a corduroy pants suit came in with a gift for her. "Oh, you should wait till I make you rich before you give me presents," she said. The girl grinned.

Mrs. Ford and I went into her pleasant, unbusinesslike office. It has large windows overlooking the entrance to the Queensborough Bridge—not a pretentious part of the city. Indeed, nothing about the Ford Agency is pretentious, and it is the right setting for Mrs. Ford. Her charm has little to do with makeup, more with health and outspokenness. Sometimes she cocks her head as she talks, and her blue eyes are animated against a skin tanned from skiing. She seems to believe that common sense is more convincing than argument, and her hit-the-nail-on-the-head questions are often intended to answer themselves.

"I hope you're not expecting to hear a tale of lost youth and tragic misunderstandings," she began. "You won't get it from me. All this business of kids trying desperately to find themselves is greatly overrated. We spend so much time trying to figure out what their motivations are. As far as I'm concerned, the only thing I was ever motivated by at age sixteen was fear. I didn't stay out later than I was allowed and I didn't come home with poor grades, simply because I would have been afraid to disobey my parents. I don't know what vague fears I had; I was never beaten and my parents were very kind to me. I didn't feel misunderstood, and I didn't brood about not being able to communicate with them. I just respected them, and for that reason I was pretty obedient. No problem. I thought my parents were rather old and quite boring, but then why shouldn't they be?

"Oh, we did wild things, of course. One of my brothers once shot out all the lights in the village with a BB gun, just to pass the time. He got into terrible trouble. My parents were furious. But you have to remember that in those days you were considered pranksterish for pulling stunts like that. Today it would qualify you as a juvenile delinquent. I singlehandedly replaced half the signs on the North Shore of Long Island from one estate to another, so if you were going to the Pratts', you wound up at the Coes', and vice versa. It was one of the greatest achievements of my sixteenth year. Furthermore, I did it with boys who are now presidents and chairmen of the board of large corporations. Today we would have been considered disturbed children and psychiatrists would undoubtedly be doing long studies about our behavior.

"I don't know why we did it. Probably just because we were sixteen. I didn't do it when I was eighteen or when I was fifteen, but at the age of sixteen we suddenly became mobile. We had cars, and we could go out and explore the world around us; and if part of that exploration was replacing estate signs, well, that's the way it was. My great ambition then was simply to go to as many college house parties as I could possibly get to before I was too old—twenty. I was also concerned with getting the best sun tan on the North Shore. I was never going to *be* anything.

"It's odd, but I almost never thought about the world around me in any real way. When Pearl Harbor was bombed, I didn't even know the Japanese were mad at us, and I was already at Barnard College, seventeen years old. God knows what I was doing—having fun, I guess.

"I loved to collect musicians. I knew lots of them and I used to just adore them. Fortunately they were very kind to me. I guess they thought they should be nice to anyone that square and adoring. I used to go into New York with my friends and just stand in front of bands. And, yes, another thing I collected was sweaters. It was my ambition to have more Monroe sweaters and McMullen dresses than anybody I knew. One thing is sure, I didn't have any desire to work or have a career. I was horrified at the thought my mother might force me to go to college, which she eventually did.

"If I could have gone to Stanford, I wouldn't have minded the idea of college at all, but my mother thinks there are Indians west of Princeton, and I never had a prayer. She took me to Barnard, and that's where I went. Then my life began to alter. Gradually I became aware of other things besides band-leaders and sweater collections.

"But at sixteen, during my last year of high school, I was very content and very confident. I had everything it took to make me, Eileen Otte, happy. My parents thought I was fine. I had reasonable marks, nice clothes and a car, a home where I could give a party every week, plenty of boyfriends. I wasn't skinny and I wasn't fat, I had no skin problems. I was just me. There was none of this problem of wondering 'Who am I?' which we hear about so endlessly now. None of my friends had identity problems, either. I didn't know any lost teenagers. We all had perfectly marvelous lives.

"I just can't believe all the sad tales I hear from people about how miserable they were as teenagers. It's become fashionable now to deprecate everything, but after all, why be a loser? So much better to be positive. It has never occurred to me that I'm wrong in my basic approach to life. I guess I'm just a very positive person.

"Of course, I'll grant that you can never know what's going on beneath the surface, but to all outward appearances my friends seemed both happy and sure of themselves. You know, I think we take the world much too seriously now, and of all the things we take too seriously, children head the list. Does it all have to be so deadly earnest? My parents had never heard of children going to psychiatrists. They would have quailed at the thought. The way they saw it, you told your kids what to do and they did it. I'm not sure but what that wasn't the best way. At least it was free of parlor-psychology techniques.

"Take one of my plans at fifteen, for example: I was going to run away on a Greyhound bus and see everything. I had collected all the pamphlets, and I really planned to do it. My family was never terribly travel-minded—if it wasn't New York or Lake Placid or Florida it didn't exist—and I always wanted to see a city like Pittsburgh or Chicago. I knew there had to be another kind of world somewhere. Was I disturbed or alienated? No, I just wanted to see other places. If a kid today did that, can you imagine the soul-searching, the concern it would arouse?

"But I never did go, I can't remember why. Probably one of my many engagements, I guess, although they were never very binding affairs. I was engaged eleven times, but all it really depended on was whose fraternity pin happened to be on the outside of the sweater I was wearing." Mrs. Ford threw back her head and laughed and laughed. "Oh, I was terrible, terrible, completely faithless.

"I read and read when I was sixteen, probably never less than a book a week. I loved history and travel books, and I gobbled up historical novels and adventure stories. Even today I can tell you all about the crocodiles in the Nile and where head-hunters hang out. I was a prodigious reader, but not a serious one. History was the only academic subject I could pursue with any deep interest. I particularly loved ancient history, because of the enormity of the problems those people solved. They fascinated me as people because their achievements were really miraculous. Now we may send someone to the moon, and that's really *quelque chose;* but I used to listen to Buck Rogers on the radio, and I always knew we'd get there—we have all the instruments. But those old Abyssinians and Babylonians, Greeks and Romans were incredible.

"My mother wanted me to be a lawyer, I never knew exactly why, but that was definitely her ambition for me. I should say right away that she was very understanding for the most part. She always saw that I had the things I needed. I could grab anyone and bring him to dinner at a moment's notice. My parents had fun together, I was aware of that, and it affected all of us in a good way.

"My father was a great sports fan and he turned me into one too. I remember picking up a great enthusiasm for track from him, and one of the most thrilling things I ever saw back then was Bill Bonthron breaking the mile record in 1939. And Ace Parker, he was one of my biggest heroes. He was captain of the football Dodgers and I thought he was the greatest man who ever lived. Musicians, athletes and film stars, they were my heroes. I loved Jimmy Stewart with a passion it's hard to believe. I was his devoted slave. When *Gone with the Wind* played, though, Clark Gable replaced him on the spot. He was number one. I still love movies and the theater, but I only go to musical comedies. I don't like serious dramas because I don't enjoy sitting in a theater and crying. I don't mind crying at the opera, though, for some reason. You can add Glenn Miller to this list as perhaps my all-time favorite, and there you have my heroes. Not very profound, is it?

"I didn't even know who was President when I was sixteen. I guess Franklin Roosevelt, but it would never have occurred to me to idolize a political figure. My knowledge of current events when I was a teenager extended to knowing that I couldn't go to Europe because of Hitler. I was furious. I guess you could say Hitler was the only person who ever curtailed me from doing what I wanted when I was sixteen.

"I entered Barnard College not really caring what I studied and possessing only one useful talent in the world. I could knit. I was really a champion knitter. My mother used to get impatient at the number of sweaters I wanted to buy, but she didn't mind if I made them myself, so I learned to knit argyles and sweaters until you'd think I was trying to use up the wool supply of the world. Anyway, I majored in political science and I didn't dislike it and I didn't have a burning desire to be a lawyer, either. But I would have made a terrible lawyer—I'm very illogical. I just sort of went along with things, but with an important difference: I learned to think. I began to grow up.

"There is absolutely no substitute," she added matter-of-factly, "for the kind of growing-up process you go through at a really first-class college. You are with people who are interested in the world around them in the most immediate sort of way. It necessitates your growing up.

"In a way I just drifted when I got out of school. I had lots of jobs because I had eloped and my husband and I were very young and very poor. I had one terrible job rationing priorities for American Export, and then I became a stylist and all-around secretary for a photographer. I ran errands and typed things—badly—and messed up the bookkeeping beyond all repair, but the point is I got the job as a stylist without any experience whatsoever. I just said I could do it, and I could—all for the grand sum of $35 a week. I used to have to mail the film to Eastman Kodak in Rochester, New York, and I'd go down into the underground concourse at Radio City every day. There was a talking myna bird there, and he and Charles, the doorman, were my best friends. But I was a career girl, right?

"Well, I worked for Arnold Constable as a copywriter, and later in the advertising and photography department. When I started this agency I was only twenty-one, and my husband and I were expecting a baby and we were broke. I knew a lot of models and I sort of rounded them up and that's how it started. I'm sorry it couldn't be more dramatic.

"My husband runs this whole place; he does all the financial part. I'm just an agent, but he's very clever. He has a marvelous sense of order and finance. Were it left to me, we'd have been out of business the first day we started. I don't care about money. It doesn't interest me except that I like to make it for people. Money is very hard to understand, so I don't bother with it.

"I *care* about my models' careers, that's what I really care about. I've got a total absorption in it. I care about this business so much it's difficult to describe, and it's a very nice business. It enables you to do things for people. Probably if I weren't a model agent, I'd be a social worker. It's a very rewarding feeling to know you've helped girls through college. Oh, sure, lots of girls go through college on what they make with us in the summer. And then I get invitations to their children's weddings, or I see them getting married to nice boys and see them start another life. It's wonderful.

"Of course the work is interesting for the models, too. It's never the same—every job is a different dress or a different coat—imagine wearing the nicest dresses! And modeling is certainly lucrative. For example, four of my girls earn upwards of $75,000 a year. They work for about ten to twelve years, which is fine. Many women would like to retire anyway by then to raise a family and have a home. Also, the demand of business is for youth."

"Do you think men like the way models look?" I asked.

"I'm not at all interested in what appeals to men. Why should I be? They don't print fashion magazines for men, do they? It's a matter of sublime indifference to me what the men of America think. My business is selling girls who can project an image of current fashion and make clothes appealing. Women don't like women who are going to compete with them. I think it's part of our Puritan heritage. Sexy women aren't really regarded by other women as *genteel*, are they? They're not, they're repugnant to other women. Like those pin-up girls—we don't have anything to do with them. Tell your young-men-about-town not to look here for their fun and games.

"Models are girls, and their lives are basically the same as other girls'. There is the difference in their looks, of course, and in the clothes that they wear modeling. A model may be a gem of sophistication to the photographer, but when she takes off the sable coat and the emeralds, she's another young girl going home very tired from having worked like a stevedore. What are they tired from? Well, they're tired from having stood on their feet all day with every muscle stretched from end to end. They're bent like pretzels.

"Hopefully, a model will have appointments scheduled all day long. It's a half-hour and a taxi, maybe twenty minutes to freshen makeup between appointments. That's why there's really no such thing as different makeup for a model for street wear. Models have to keep the same makeup on all day because it's just impossible to put on full makeup in the half-hour between appointments. To start from scratch with makeup, from a thorough cleansing on, takes a good two hours, so usually they wear big glasses to hide their eyes.

"It's physical qualifications that lead girls to model different types of clothes. A junior is about five foot five to five foot seven, she weighs from, maybe, ninety-five to one hundred pounds. She looks like a typical American teenager, that's all. She has to look normal. Normal can mean anyone. We have Jewish and Negro models, but there should be no definite characteristics about them, that's what I mean by normal. They can't look too Latin or too Jewish or too Swedish or too this or that. They have to look like nobody—do you understand?—or everybody.

"Then you get to another model group that does sportswear. They are college-type, young-housewife-type girls. They must be five foot seven to five foot eight and weigh from about one hundred and five to one hundred and sixteen pounds. They must look just like sporty young housewives or college girls.

"And finally, high fashion. That's the ultimate, that's everybody's dream. The pay is the same, but girls just like to wear those clothes. So would I. It must be fun to be swathed in sables and ermines, to have a hairdresser fixing your hair every twelve seconds. They get to work for the really slick magazines, *Vogue* and *Bazaar,* and they earn $40 to $60 an hour, $40 to start. But nobody wants them at $40, so they just have to pot around until they get going. High-fashion models are tall, five foot eight to five foot nine and a half, and they weigh from one hundred fifteen to one hundred and twenty-four pounds. They weigh more, of course, because they're taller.

"But basically all models have wide-set, large eyes. Mainly they have straight noses, mouths that aren't thick or thin, long necks, long arms, thin long hands, thin legs and gigantic feet. Yes, gigantic feet. They do, they have astonishingly large feet. I suppose they need them to hold them up all day, although I believe the shoe business is still using size 4B."

Mrs. Ford was interrupted by an attractive blond girl who came in suddenly to ask a question. They spoke for several minutes. Although an employee, the girl might have been taken for a model herself. The receptionist had also been pretty and unaffected. I had learned from her that girls wishing to model with the agency are usually interviewed mornings, and several candidates were in the waiting room—a lovely French girl in a pink dress, an icy blond in an all-fluff coat and knee-high, lace-up boots. Through a closing door I had glimpsed one working Ford model, a willowy brunette with a hooked nose.

The Ford agency is a world of women, and when Mrs. Ford was free, I asked if there were many men in the business and if models could meet them through their work.

"It's difficult to meet men in the modeling business," she replied. "Where do you meet them? Photographers? There are only a limited number of photographers, and some of those are married. That leaves very few to go around, and the people in the trade don't take out models; it's just not good business. Unless a model has girlfriends, who can help, she comes to the city and she's all alone.

"Models have to concentrate on themselves; they can't eat too much, and they must always eat the right food. And models can't stay out all night every night (but oh, I love to stay out all night, just sort of stomp around). My job is basically to try to tell my girls what's right for them. There's no point in just telling them what's wrong, is there? But the shortest distance between two points is just a very straight line—isn't it?—so there's no point in sentimentalizing over it. What you must instill in a girl is not self-vanity, but a very cold-blooded eye. I'm not coldhearted, I'm helpful."

Mrs. Ford likes people, and clearly that is part of the fun for her of being where she is. Another part is an equally personal liking for fashion, which she began to talk about.

"If fashions didn't change, we'd all die of boredom. Wouldn't it be awful to wear the same dress forever? Well, anyway, it keeps me in the business, and besides, there'd be no reason for fashion magazines. I get a definite pleasure from reading them. You can get lots of magazines devoted to everything else, but fashion is essentially for women a moment of escape from the humdrum lives they might lead. Not everybody's interested in book reviews or politics.

"I love clothes. I like to think about them, and they are a

large part of my life. To me there's nothing nicer than thinking about what I'll be wearing in the spring. I've ordered three dresses, and I look forward to them and I'll wait for them. Just like my father, he looked forward to football and baseball. So clothes are for me a way of life, and they are for most women. Besides, there has to be something for everyone. What if we all wanted the same thing? I'm dying to go to Lord & Taylor's and see those bathing suits they advertised in the *Times*. If you like one-piece bathing suits, you'd like them.

"And liking clothes isn't a matter of having a lot of money. Any girl can dress the way she wants to if she goes to the right store. To me, fashion is a departure from the reality of working all day, every day. I think it is for most women, for housewives in particular. It must be awful to do that all the time without any release. Hasn't it been proven now that if women do only housework, they begin to resent it?

"I have four children myself," she said, "so it isn't as if I don't know something about being a mother and a housewife."

I asked her whether any of her children looked forward to a career in modeling.

"One is almost twenty and she's almost up to five foot four, so that eliminates her as a model. Besides, I think she'll be a curator in a museum, which is what she wants to do. I have a son fourteen, who really only cares about skiing and tennis. And I've a daughter eleven. She thinks that makeup is dreadful, in capital letters. Then I have a daughter who is nine who thinks the whole thing is great, so we'll see.

"All my children are great athletes. My eleven-year-old wants to be an Olympic swimmer, possibly a skier. Considering that I can't even play tiddlywinks, it's a miracle."

Mrs. Ford paused, then abruptly summed up her feelings about the whole subject. "Self-confidence—that's the most important gift you can have. That's *it*, really, don't you think? Self-confidence, whether women look their greatest or think they look their greatest, so long as they believe in themselves. Of course I'm an optimist, a tremendous optimist, because I don't see how anybody as darling as me could ever fail.

"And probably that idea came from my mother and father, don't you think?" she added.

Margaret Mead

*Margaret Mead was born December 16, 1901, the daughter
of Edward Sherwood Mead, an economist, and Emily Fogg
Mead, a sociologist. As a girl, she often heard talk at home
about the social sciences and now says that is probably why
she became an anthropologist. She was educated at home in
Doylestown, Pennsylvania, until her teens, when she attended
Doylestown High School and New Hope School for Girls. After
one year at De Pauw University in Chicago, she transferred to
Barnard College in New York City, graduating in 1923. She
received her master's degree in psychology (1924) and a doctorate in anthropology (1929), both from Columbia University.*

[85]

*As an anthropologist, Dr. Mead made oceanic ethnology her specialty. She studied and lived among the Polynesians of Samoa (1925), in the Admiralty Islands (1928–29), New Guinea (1931–33), Bali (1936–38) and New Guinea (1936–39, 1953, 1964–65). Her books about these field trips—*Coming of Age in Samoa, Growing Up in New Guinea, Sex and Temperament in Three Primitive Societies *and* From the South Seas, *among others—have been described as "an extraordinary subtle performance." Much of her work is now in paperback and is, as well, required reading at colleges and universities.*

*For most of her professional life, Dr. Mead has been associated with the American Museum of Natural History; but her interests have ranged far beyond strictly academic anthropology. She is considered a specialist in education and culture, mental health, family life, and cross-national relationships. Her recent books show an increasing concern with modern culture (*And Keep Your Powder Dry, Soviet Attitudes Towards Authority) *and with the workings of her own discipline (*An Anthropologist at Work, Anthropologists and What They Do). *She frequently contributes on these and other subjects to national magazines.*

Dr. Mead's work has earned her numerous awards including fifteen honorary degrees, the Woman of the Year Award (1957) and the presidency of the World Federation of Mental Health (1956–57). She is frequently invited to lecture at universities and colleges in this country and abroad.

Margaret Mead has one daughter, Mary Catherine Bateson Kassarjian, an accomplished linguist.

In An Anthropologist at Work, *Dr. Mead describes vividly what it was like to study anthropology in the early 1920's. The Department of Anthropology at Columbia University was then virtually a one-professor department. Dr. Franz Boas taught every course; his assistant was Ruth Benedict, who later wrote the classic* Patterns of Culture; *and Margaret Mead, then twenty years old and a student at Barnard College, was an avid beginner. Students had to be enthusiastic because Dr. Boas taught with "dreadful concentration . . . plunging directly into the analysis of difficult American Indian languages."*

It was a "small, embattled group at Columbia," Dr. Mead writes, and a critical period for anthropology itself. Traditionalists pored doggedly over technical facts, and the notion that an anthropologist's method—like the decision to live among the natives—might be significant or creative was unheard-of. Then, in 1925, Dr. Boas sent Margaret Mead on a field trip to Samoa, because he thought it was "time to attack a new set of problems." Her trip and the findings that came out of it are described in Coming of Age in Samoa, *published in 1928. The book is one of the first examples of the radically new direction anthropology has since taken. Margaret Mead lived among the Polynesians as one of themselves, and her method was crucial. In descriptions of South Sea Island girls, she showed that different societies produce very different styles of human behavior.*

Margaret Mead

Dr. Margaret Mead's offices at the American Museum of
Natural History are two practically attic rooms on the sixth
floor of the graystone museum that occupies several blocks on
Central Park West in New York City. I took an elevator to the
fifth floor, which is not open to the public, and then found the
way, along confusing corridors, to the stairway to the sixth.

As I searched for Dr. Mead's office, I explored a little. I
found a large cardboard carton full of life-size plaster-of-Paris
ape heads; a handful of crusty, reddish Mexican Quetzalcoatls;
and, at the foot of the stairway to Dr. Mead's office, a huge old
plowing wagon with solid wooden wheels.

I climbed the stairway. From somewhere on the sixth floor
came the sound of typing. Crates were piled to the ceiling. Dr.
Mead's office, when I found it, was on the left. It was a long,
high-ceilinged room furnished with a great table almost as long
as the room. At the far end of the table, near the windows, Dr.
Mead was already working. There is a second, smaller office for

[89]

her secretaries, two pretty college-age girls. Dr. Mead likes to have a number of college students working around her.

Both are real workrooms. The smaller one is brimful of boxes, wire baskets and filing cabinets, all carefully labeled. (One of Dr. Mead's rules of thumb is "always write everything down.") But it must be a pleasant place to work. It is under the eaves, with part of a window showing nine feet up on the wall. White Japanese lanterns hang from the rafters and bright yellow papers, scribbled over in Magic Marker, are tacked here and there.

Dr. Mead's answer to my first question a few minutes later was a warm and sudden: "Of course I remember my sixteenth year. When I was sixteen, people said I didn't have a sense of humor. I don't know whether they meant it as some form of abuse or not, but that's what they said."

She smiled from a perennially young face. She wears her hair bobbed and carefree, and although it is gray now, she looks almost as she did at twenty-three in a photograph, which she showed me, taken of herself in Samoa. She is small and sturdy, and in the photograph I at first took her for a South Sea Islander because of a short, bowl-cropped haircut. Illustration and documentation are second nature to her and a number of times she carefully pointed up what she was saying with photographs and book references.

"I was like young people today, precocious," she continued. "I put my hair up at twelve and wore skirts longer than was customary. Putting your hair up then was very significant. It meant you regarded yourself as an adult. Well, I was anxious to be an adult. I thought life was more interesting for adults. My mother's friends would raise eyebrows over my skirts but I was allowed to wear them. My mother never begrudged my having my own way. She was both open-minded and radical.

She ardently supported woman's suffrage, Consumers League, higher taxes and better education."

Dr. Mead paused and, apparently with some wonder still, added, "Then, when I was sixteen, I realized that I was the baby of the class by two years and this could be fun."

I asked if she had felt the effects of being precocious in school. She had, partly because her entire family was unusually "self-conscious about education. My father was an economist, and my mother was herself a social scientist." I was astonished when she added that her formal schooling until high school consisted only of "two years of kindergarten and half a day in the fourth grade." "Half a day," she explained, "was quite enough for me to realize that I knew what they were teaching already. I would have been bored had I stayed, and besides my parents disapproved of the educational system in general, of children spending long, boring hours at school. So for the intermediate years, I was educated at home. My grandmother, who had been a teacher, gave me an hour's lesson a day, and the rest of the time I spent outdoors or reading by myself.

"Of course, it is still true today—that schools bore many children. Why should we send children to school to learn how to read, for example? They should already know how to read by that age. We don't send children to school to learn how to walk, do we? It's different if the child's family speaks a foreign language or can't read and write. *That* child has to go to school to learn to read. But otherwise, why should children be obliged to sit still all day and pretend to be raptly interested in what they already know."

When Dr. Mead did go to formal school, "I would get restless," she said. "My parents tried to find me schools that were different and more stimulating. Once I went to a girls' private school that was very precious." (She repeated "very

precious," and I gathered she meant "somewhat artificial.")
"There were six teachers and fourteen pupils," she added.

"In the high school from which I graduated, German was
discontinued with the coming of World War I, out of mistaken
patriotism. As a result, I was short the language credits I
needed to be accepted at college. I had had only two years of
German and four of Latin." So in order to get her college
entrance, she said, she compressed three years of French into
one.

"In high school, when I was fifteen and sixteen, I was very
active in extracurricular activities. I went around with a small
crowd of about sixteen boys and girls, organized clubs, did
public speaking, and senior year was an editor of the high
school paper which I had helped to start the year before." She
reached to a bookshelf behind her for a pamphlet to show me a
poem she had written at fifteen, as a junior, for the senior class.
After reciting the names of the ancient great, it ended:

> On your shoulders falls their mantle
> Settling light as a caress.
> Will you answer, heirs of ages
> Saint and sages—we say "yes!"

"At sixteen, everything seemed possible," she said with no
trace of nostalgia and as if she still thought so. Later, at
Barnard College, she wrote more poetry and used to work with
her teacher, Ruth Benedict, on both anthropology and poetry.
"But my own poems were hardly ever good enough to submit
even to tiny magazines."

Dr. Mead likes to hold close to whatever subject she is
talking about, and she returned to her sixteenth year: "I was
sixteen in 1917," she said precisely, "the first year of United
States' involvement in World War I, and of course that affected
all our lives. After school in the afternoons I went to the Red

Cross to help make bandages for the war effort. They didn't have machines to make them then. During the summer of 1918 I read aloud current books about the war to my two grand-mothers. Eventually I even learned to turn the heel of a sock while I was reading.

"During the war you couldn't get servants," she added. "We had to make do on the farm without them. Try and realize what that meant. There were eighteen rooms, and that meant eighteen kerosene lights. That summer I did all the family cooking, too. But I thought it was important to *learn* the homemaking skills before marrying and raising a family. I did the entire washing once for the same reason, to see how it was done. I feel the same way today: I would never administer a psychological test without having taken it first myself to see what it involved."

She showed me a photograph of herself at sixteen. The lace sleeves of the dress in the photograph had been her mother's, "when she was a graduate student at Bryn Mawr. I remember I felt very good wearing that dress. I did enjoy my sixteenth year. We had dances at home every Saturday night. You had to know sixteen or seventeen dances to be considered at all accomplished. We did tangos and Latin American dances.

"I was in love at sixteen, too. But of course, I didn't dream of being married any time soon. In 1914, one didn't think of such early marriage. Not that I advocate girls waiting until they are thirty-five or forty years old, but girls should have more time to discover what it is to be a woman.

"Love, I feel, needs distance and tension. I very seldom see lovers today. Dating every night in junior high school is just part of a competitive game that has little to do with love, or even with sex. Love needs distance, and I believe young lovers should be apart for some of the time, several years anyway. It necessitates letter-writing, and there ought to be more letter-writing.

"At sixteen, I wrote a four-page letter every night to my fiancé. He was in the army, stationed at Fort Knox. The first two pages had to be something completely new—I wouldn't allow myself to plan them in advance—and that habit helped me later on my lecture tours in England during World War II. I made it a policy then to bill the first half-hour of the lecture for something I had learned in the last twenty-four hours. The letters between my fiancé and myself were filled with thoughts and ideas, which was our idea of romance."

I asked Dr. Mead if she remembered ever feeling rebellious as a sixteen-year-old. She did not, except "I joined the Episcopal Church." She explained: "That may not seem particularly rebellious, but in the context of my family it was. My mother always listed herself in *Who's Who* as an agnostic, so she was terribly against my church interests. It was very funny—I remember her claiming children always caught contagious diseases at Sunday school, apparently *only* at Sunday school, not day school. Joining the church was a form of rebellion, a search for my own identity by going into the past. In some ways it was less troublesome, and it was harder for my parents to grapple with.

"The only instance of typical adolescent unhappiness that I can remember did not occur over something that happened to me. But when my favorite godmother broke her engagement, I don't know who was more miserable, she or I. I remember standing on a lonely road at sunset thinking it was the end of everything. That was the only unhappiness I had. I mean unhappiness that was not situational, that developed out of a mood. No, perhaps not, for I suppose that was situational too.

"You see for me at sixteen the choice was never a question of 'Who am I,' but of 'What am I going to do?' I had to choose whether I wanted an activist life or not. If I hadn't been born into my family, perhaps I might have looked forward solely to being a homemaker and wife. I remember at the time I did want six children—that was my ideal. But within the context of my family other things seemed open to me as well. I never saw any discrepancy between the things of the mind and marriage. It never occurred to me that they were incompatible. I simply assumed that a woman could have both.

"For a while I hoped to be a painter—I had some talent—but then I was told that someone who wanted to be a painter could not go to college. I gave up painting then. My grandmother and my mother before me had been to college. It was something I had always expected to do.

"One of the things that made me choose anthropology were my teachers, Franz Boas and Ruth Benedict. I first met Ruth Benedict when I was a senior at Barnard College in the autumn of 1922. Of course she was older—she began her graduate work at thirty-three—but she was also very shy and inarticulate then, and I was almost her contemporary in anthropology. I began my anthropological work in the year in which she took her Ph.D. So she was really a student-teacher, although she had experience in other fields that I lacked."

When Dr. Mead went on her first field trip, to Samoa, where she lived in a Samoan village, she was only twenty-three years old. I asked if the experience had frightened her. "Not personally," she said, "but I was afraid I wouldn't be able to do the research I'd been sent to do. I hadn't even been to Europe before I went." She added, "I went to Samoa on one of the first National Research grants ever offered in this country.

The program was so new at the time that they worried about advancing me money for two months in a place as far away as Samoa. Perhaps they thought I might abscond.

"When I arrived, I stayed in a hotel in Pago Pago for six weeks to learn the language, then I went out and lived in a village. Learning to speak the language wasn't as difficult as getting used to Samoan food. I learned to eat it, though— breadfruit, bananas, fish, land crabs. The staple, taro, is a tuber. It tastes a little like Ivory soap. But soon after I had learned all this, there was a hurricane and we were fed by the Red Cross on rice and canned salmon.

"The Samoans gave me several titles—one was Flower of Heaven. The girls in the village treated me like one of themselves, perhaps partly because I was small. I was five foot two and weighed ninety-nine pounds. The Samoans are larger and buxom. But then if I chose I could go to another village and say, 'I'm writing a book,' and they would respond to me as if I were quite serious and old and scholarly." I asked Dr. Mead what she wore in Samoa. "I wore my own calico dresses," she said, "but if there was a ceremonial, they dressed me up Samoan-style," and she showed me a photograph of herself, standing between two Polynesian girls, in the handwoven dress "made by the last queen of the island, whose name, like mine, was Makelita."

Dr. Mead is famous for her comparisons of different cultures, and I asked if she could compare sixteen-year-old Samoan girls with herself at sixteen, or with sixteen-year-olds today. In *Coming of Age in Samoa,* she tells the stories of girls—of Pele, Tita, the Luma clique and others—with such immediacy that the reader realizes every girl in any culture has her own problems and personality. This one is jealous of her older, prettier sister; this one has to work too hard at home to have much fun. "But the American girl's problems are more complex," Dr. Mead said simply. "The Samoans were content."

Of this country, she added, "I think in many ways the Twenties in America were similar to the Sixties. It was a young and hopeful world in the 1920's. So much seemed capable of rapid solution. The mood was activist, as it is today with the Peace Corps, CORE, sit-ins—all forms of action. And in the Twenties we were concerned, as they are now, with being individuals. The Fifties were different—the Dismal Fifties— until young people came to life again with an interest in civil rights. The focus today is immediacy, do something now."

I asked Dr. Mead if she had any thoughts about the current interest among young people in the use of drugs and LSD.

"I think LSD is an example of the urgency with which young people want things now, at once," she answered. "A trip to Japan is much better than an LSD trip, but a boy can't go to Japan this minute, or tomorrow, so he takes LSD. LSD is also a form of anti-alcoholism. I mean, drinking is considered wicked, as by the standards of our Puritan heritage it always has been. But I doubt if anyone will ever have a spiritual experience solely on LSD, any more than he would necessarily have a vision just from walking in the desert.

"A most important responsibility for young people today is to try to understand their own times. And that can't be done without communication between generations, which shows the relationship of new and old knowledge to one's own life. I don't believe in ivory towers. Today parents pressure their children into premature adulthood—'Keep up with others.' It's unfortunate that American boys and girls are so focused on their contemporaries. They ought to look to larger heroes, too.

"But most of all, a sixteen-year-old girl needs time to live, to simply be. And she needs more friends from among her own

[97]

sex. In Samoa the girls went around for years almost exclusively with other girls. Dating the opposite sex every night isn't very helpful. It's from their own sex that girls find out who they are. In all great civilizations, it has been customary for boys to grow up in the company of other boys—in schools, colleges, the military—but this has never been formulated for girls."

Dr. Mead talked enthusiastically; indeed the lives and reactions of young people have been a subject of keen interest to her throughout her career. She mentioned *Keep Your Powder Dry*, a book on changing American society, and noted: "The highest compliment I ever received on this book was implicit in a question asked by a slightly aggrieved adolescent: 'How did Margaret Mead know how my mother brought me up?'" But how *did* she, I wondered, since her own sixteenth year had not been troubled. She herself has given several answers: that she has always felt keenly the sense of being a woman and therefore has directed much of her research to the study of children; that she hoped, by describing education in Samoa and other far-off countries, to throw light on America's educational system. But perhaps the best answer is something Ruth Benedict once said about her in a letter: "Margaret lives intensely in the outer world."

It was with this spirit of constructive optimism that Dr. Mead described the future for today's sixteen-year-olds. "Of course the young can have an impact on their culture," she said emphatically. "And to know something about what the future will bring, you have only to ask, 'How old will the sixteen-year-old of today be in the year 2000? How old will he or she be in 2020?' The future will be what she makes of it."

Bette Davis

Bette Davis has been one of America's most distinguished actresses for over thirty years. Among her more than eighty films have been some of the most notable to come out of Holly-wood: The Petrified Forest, Dark Victory, The Private Lives of Elizabeth and Essex, All This and Heaven Too, The Letter, The Little Foxes, Of Human Bondage, All About Eve, Jezebel. *She has created a memorable gallery of characters: a vulgar Cock-ney waitress in* Of Human Bondage; *a dominating queen in* The Private Lives of Elizabeth and Essex; *an aging, cynical actress in* All About Eve; *and, most recently, the dotty, driven women of* Whatever Happened to Baby Jane? *and* Hush, Hush, Sweet Charlotte. *She has won two Academy Awards (for* Dangerous *in 1935,* Jezebel *in 1938) and has been President of the Academy of Motion Picture Arts and Sciences.*

She was born Ruth Elizabeth Davis on April 5, 1908, in Lowell, Massachusetts. Her father, Harlow Morrell Davis, was a lawyer; her mother, "Ruthie" as Bette Davis affectionately calls her, was a woman of limitless energy and lucky hunches. When her parents were divorced in 1916, Mrs. Davis became a free-lance photographer to support herself and her two daughters, Bette and younger sister, "Bobbie." The three moved from place to place in New England, and once to New York City. Bette and Bobbie attended a boarding school in the Berkshires, Newton High School outside of Boston, a New York City public school, and finally Cushing Academy in Ashburnham, Massachusetts, where Miss Davis graduated.

After some fledgling attempts at high school plays, Bette Davis and Ruthie, too, decided she should try seriously for a theatrical career. Miss Davis's mother marched into John Murray Anderson's Dramatic School in New York City and convinced him to give Bette a scholarship. Bette Davis's first major role, in The Earth Between *at the Provincetown Playhouse, came as the result of one of Ruthie's hunches: "Understudy the role of Pearl," she said. "The actress playing that part is going to have an accident." So it happened, and Bette Davis, who had learned the part by heart, went on instead. Later, she toured in Ibsen's* The Wild Duck *(just barely making rehearsal after a bout of mumps); and in 1929 she appeared for the first time on Broadway in* Broken Dishes. *Another Broadway performance, in* Solid South *in 1930, brought her a screen test and a contract from Universal Pictures.*

It was not easy going in Hollywood at the start. Miss Davis learned how to act for movies, which she discovered was quite different from acting on the stage, by haunting movie houses and watching. *At first, as she tells in her autobiography,* The Lonely Life, *directors did not see her potential: she was frequently cast as the mousy "good sister," and her attempts to bring realism to the screen—to look ill, for example, in a hospital take—were rejected. Not until she appeared in* Of Human Bondage *in 1934 was her talent, and her public appeal recognized. Thereafter she rose quickly to stardom, though she still could not always get the roles she wanted. Vivian Leigh, for example, became Scarlett O'Hara in* Gone with the Wind. *This was a part Bette Davis wanted desperately.*

In 1932, Miss Davis married a classmate from Cushing Academy, Harmon Oscar Nelson, Jr. But, as in her later three marriages, she found it difficult to reconcile a career with marriage, and the Nelsons were divorced in 1938. By her third marriage, to artist William Grant Sherry, she has one daughter, Barbara. She and Gary Merrill, her fourth husband, adopted two children, Michael and Margo.

Miss Davis is renowned for a flash-fire temper and an assertive independence of spirit. When she felt she was being overlooked in Hollywood despite the success of Baby Jane, *she took an advertisement in a Hollywood trade paper: "Mother of three . . . divorcée, American. Thirty years experience as an actress . . . wants steady employment in Hollywood."*

She is proud of her success and of the hard work that went into it. "The person who wants to make it," she says, "has to sweat. There are no short cuts. And you've got to have the guts to be hated. That's the hardest part."

Bette Davis

AT SIXTEEN I had very pink cheeks and long blond hair. Mother made all my clothes in the style of the day, and my hair was dressed in a Marcel wave, which was fashionable then. I was a bouncy sixteen-year-old."

This was Bette Davis talking, not to an audience in a movie theater, but to me, in a cottage in Westport, Connecticut, as I ate a bowl of pea soup that she had cooked and served. It was delicious soup.

The theater and drama were present, however. Her voice is compelling; her gestures have a dramatic quality. She has a whooping laugh, happy or derisive. Her responses are sudden, snappy, no-nonsense. Most dominant are the eyes—crystally turquoise, warm, yet wary and discerning.

The cottage was very pleasant and rustic. The windows around three sides of the living room gave a view of grass and bare earth, clumps of pine trees and an old barn painted red. The slip covers on the couch were a floral design of large morning glories. On one side of the room, a Franklin stove puffed away, demanding periodic stoking and fresh logs. Miss Davis wore simple country clothes—a beige sweater, plaid skirt, white knitted stockings and suede, boot-type shoes.

"This cottage belongs to the Albert Browns," Miss Davis said. "I rent it from them. I met Mrs. Brown when I was sixteen in Ogunquit, Maine. There are only a few people you remain friends with through the years.

"When I was sixteen I attended Cushing Academy in Ashburnham, Massachusetts. My mother went to the same school when she was sixteen. Not among the great chic Yankee schools, but a very charming coed school. Actually, I'm not sure I really believe in coeducational schools. Possibly in the college years, but in high school I think it's too distracting. I remember at Cushing, every spring our marvelous headmaster, Dr. Cowell, would give us a talk about 'spring fever.' 'Now, ladies and gentlemen,' he would begin, 'spring is here.' We used to roar with laughter—we knew full well what he meant.

"It was at Cushing that I learned what I think was the greatest lesson of my life. My parents were divorced, and my mother had two daughters to support with basically very little financial help. At that age I wasn't too aware of how difficult that was for her. One day the principal, Dr. Cowell, called me in and said, 'Wouldn't you like to help your mother with your tuition by waiting on tables?' I was charming and adorable: 'I'll write to her,' I said, being absolutely positive she'd refuse. Mother would *never* allow her daughter to be a waitress! But she fooled me. She said yes. I cried for about three days. Then, at six o'clock one morning, I had to go down the hill to the dining room and wait on all my friends. It wasn't fun but I did learn about people. I discovered who the worthwhile ones were in about one week. They were the ones who admired me for what I was doing. Others thought I was nothing because I was a waitress. I've always remembered this and know from that experience that it really doesn't matter what anyone does. It's what kind of a person he is.

"Well, that seems a long time ago," she said smiling. "Talking about yourself at sixteen is like talking about somebody else. You look back and it has so little to do with you now. It's like seeing the first movies you made—you think, it can't be the same person. Of course, it isn't the same person.

"Actually, I do remember what I was like at sixteen—I adored school, was a very good student, loved every minute of it. I was well-behaved, didn't have any desire to go against the rules, to be a rebel. I was popular with my classmates. I felt, also, that my life would be a special one. I had to be a leader, had to be the head of everything, and was. That causes jealousy, of course. At sixteen those who envied me called me 'stuck-up.' I never could understand that. I suppose it was because I went my own way, was independent and believed in what I was doing. I remember that the senior class willed me a box of handkerchiefs when I was a junior, to blow my 'knows' with. I wept with humiliation. I couldn't understand. Later I realized, because I wouldn't date the senior class football players, this was their revenge. I always have done what I wanted to and have allowed few people to influence me."

Miss Davis' sister, Bobbie, who lives with her, came in at that point, to show me a drawing of Lowe Hall, their dormitory at Cushing, sent to Miss Davis as a Christmas card. The picture brought a rush of reminiscences. "It hasn't changed a bit," she said. "I went back to Cushing just once, after I had become famous, for a football game. I was asked to give a kiss to every boy who made a touchdown. Those poor embarrassed guys! But it must have been some incentive, because they absolutely skunked the other team."

"You should mention that you were voted the prettiest girl in your class," Miss Davis' sister said. "Do you remember the headache band you wore?"

"That was to cover my pimples," Miss Davis said, laughing.

"I was a very gregarious person at that age. I really had a ball. But I suppose," she said wryly, "Mother could give you a different version. I know I was difficult to bring up. I had to have my own way. In the true sense of the word, I have always been temperamental. Like the weather in Maine, they say if you don't like it, wait a minute. I suppose that's because I always react strongly to what happens around me.

"I wasn't very sophisticated then. I was brought up in the traditional Yankee way. It's a Puritan upbringing. Facts aren't faced at all with young people, particularly in the area of the man-woman relationship. That's changing today. Then, the only education about sex came from the family and if they didn't care to discuss it with you, you had no means of understanding the 'facts of life.' At sixteen I was too unsophisticated to know there was a problem. Later, I made many mistakes because of my ignorance in these matters.

"I always liked guys better than girls. They were my best friends. I met my first husband, Ham, at Cushing when I was sixteen. He was a year older than I. He was the leader of the school orchestra. Actually, he paid little attention to the girls at school. This challenged me enormously—I made up my mind that I'd be his girl. Not long after, he gave me his fraternity pin. The boys and girls at Cushing were allowed to see each other very little socially. We used to signal to each other from the dorms with flashlights after lights out! Ham was a trumpet player, so he played taps for me every night. The rules were very strict. You weren't allowed to walk on campus in the rain under an umbrella because maybe you'd kiss each other. You were allowed to talk in the parlor for an hour every Sunday evening, chaperoned. Then, of course, there were the Saturday night dances. After Ham graduated he went to Massachusetts Agricultural College. We saw each other through the years—Christmas vacations, summer holidays. Ten years later we were married. At the time I was on my way as a contract player at Warner Brothers Studio in Hollywood.

"At Cushing, Ham and I had the leads in Booth Tarkington's *Seventeen.* I played Lola Pratt, a sophisticated girl from the South. I was the city girl and Ham was the country boy of seventeen, and when she, Lola, came into his life, she threw him for a loop. It's funny"—Miss Davis paused and mused— "Southern parts have followed me throughout my career."

"When did you decide to become an actress?" I asked.

"I'm not sure about that specifically, but I always knew I would do something unusual. When I was sixteen I saw Peg Entwistle in *The Wild Duck* at the Jewett Theater in Boston. From then on I dreamed about playing Hedvig a great deal, because Miss Entwistle and I looked so alike. As it turned out, Hedvig was one of the first roles I was asked to play in the theater.

"I always knew I'd never live a typical suburban life in Massachusetts. Mother was a professional photographer in order to give her two daughters the best in life. Mother, my sister and I used to call ourselves the Three Musketeers. It was my mother who made it possible for me to have a theatrical career. By working, so I could go to a dramatic school, but most of all because of her belief in my future success. Hers wasn't just a silly, stagestruck-mother kind of belief, either. I must say, the greatest pleasure out of it all was that I lived up to her belief.

"My father was opposed to the whole idea—that inspired me, too. Having somebody *against* you can help also. It's a challenge.

"I guess the first really definite beginning of my career happened the summer I was sixteen in Peterboro, New Hampshire. Mother had a photographic studio there. I spent the summer studying dancing with Roshanara at Mariarden, a school of the theater in Peterboro. Frank Conroy, one of our great American actors, was appearing nightly at the school with the Clive Players of Boston, on the stage of a professional theater connected with Mariarden. Mother asked Frank Conroy's advice about the possibility of my future in the theatrical profession. After seeing a performance of *A Midsummer Night's Dream* I gave with the other members of the dancing school in the theater at Mariarden, he told her that 'I came across the footlights,' it was not an impossible dream.

"I had a marvelous childhood. A lot of people say that actors only come from under the Brooklyn Bridge—I was fortunate that I did not. The one thing we didn't have after Mother and Daddy were divorced was a permanent home. That has its advantages, too, moving about. You learn to be adaptable, to cope. There were lots of things I had to cope with. I attended a New York public school one year. I was thirteen and the school, P. S. 186, had three thousand children. It was difficult for a girl used to a private boarding school in the country, but it was good for my future. In this school I learned about race, creed and color. As I think back, Mother gave us a most marvelous varied education for the world we went into later."

There was a knock at the door and Miss Davis got up to let in a delivery boy with groceries. About sixteen, the boy tried hard not to stare at Miss Davis, but didn't succeed. When he left, she laughed. "You've never seen such expressions when people see me in this cottage," she said. "I'm often asked, 'Do you live here all the time?' Motion-picture people are supposed to live in palaces, I guess!"

It was getting dark outside, time for me to leave. As Miss Davis walked me to the door she said: "A great deal of my life had nothing to do with Hollywood. Any time I wasn't working, I came back East. This is where I like to be."

We came out into the cool air and said goodbye. "Oh the air, smell the air," she said as I walked down the path.

Gloria Foster

Gloria Foster first became known to a wide public when she appeared in a documentary play about the American South, In White America. One of the parts she played, that of the Negro schoolgirl baited by a crowd of whites in Little Rock, Arkansas, struck close to home. "I try very hard," Miss Foster said, "not to be too realistic about a number of things. But these things that you try to forget in your past—they come back."

Born November 15, 1936, Gloria Foster was brought up by her grandparents. The family lived on the South Side of Chicago until she was seven. Then her grandfather, a laborer in a foundry, decided to become a farmer so that Gloria would not have to attend Chicago's public schools. The family moved first to Janesville, Wisconsin, then to South Beloit, Illinois. "Isn't that something," Miss Foster remarks; "he knew nothing about farming."

She never knew her father and still does not know if he is alive or dead. And she was nineteen before she found out that her mother was alive and in a mental institution. (Now her mother lives with Miss Foster's grandmother and brother and his five children. "That's the happy part," she says; "my mother lost those twenty years, but now she's well and I find her a very nice and funny lady.")

After graduation from South Beloit High School, she went to teachers college at Illinois State University. Then, at nineteen, she married and led what she calls the conservative life. But her marriage did not work out (divorce came later) and the prospect of teaching had lost its appeal. She dropped out of college a year before she would have graduated and enrolled instead in Chicago's Goodman School of Drama. There, Dr. Bella Itkin encouraged her, both personally and as an actress, and, as Miss Foster says, "changed my life."

Her first professional dramatic role was a stroke of luck: a casual acquaintance asked her to appear for two weeks in Lorraine Hansberry's A Raisin in the Sun *in Syracuse.*

In 1963–64, for her work in In White America, *Miss Foster received the Vernon Rice and Obie awards for the best performance by an actress off-Broadway. Excited by the subject of the play, she began "avidly to devour anything on Negro history, a subject which had been completely neglected in my formal education." But she did not remain typecast as a Negro and, in 1966, played* Medea *in the play, set in ancient Greece, by Robinson Jeffers. Miss Foster's strong portrayal of the tragic heroine earned her both critical praise—"olympian . . . monumental . . . a thunderclap"—and another Obie. Her next stage role was as Andromache in the Circle in the Square production of* The Trojan Women. *It was followed by a performance in the revival of Garcia Lorca's* Yerma *at Lincoln Center for the Performing Arts.*

Miss Foster has received equal acclaim for two films: The Cool World, *a semi-documentary about Negro children grow-*

ing up in the slums, and Nothing but a Man. *Early in 1967 she traveled to Africa to make a third movie,* The Comedians, *an adaptation of a Graham Greene novel, with a cast headed by Richard Burton and Elizabeth Taylor.*

She returned to the United States in late spring, 1967, to appear in the second professional production in this country of Strindberg's A Dream Play *at Chicago's Goodman Theater.*

Offstage, Miss Foster describes herself as "very much a homebody." She now lives in New York, in a three-room apartment on a quiet, tree-lined street in Greenwich Village.

Gloria Foster

GLORIA FOSTER's dressing room is hard to find in the underground labyrinth at Lincoln Center for the Performing Arts. Long, carpeted hallways lead past dozens of dressing rooms, and I had to ask directions from other actors and actresses glimpsed through half-open doors. At last I found the door labeled "Miss Foster." Most of the dressing rooms are shared, but she has her own, as befits a star. The interior is simple. A small teak box beneath a lighted mirror and a tray of fan mail are the only personal touches.

In three hours, Miss Foster would appear onstage at the Vivian Beaumont Theater in *Yerma,* a strongly emotional, tragic play in which her role keeps her stage center for the entire performance. Still, she greeted me with composure. She wore a floor-length, soft wool robe, and had a voluminous green kerchief bound around her head.

"What exactly would you like to hear about me?" she asked in a low, musical voice. "I suppose I had experiences at sixteen which don't have much bearing on anything but me. Do you want to hear about them?"

"Yes," I said so promptly that she laughed, wrinkling her nose—a laugh as quick and infectious as a girl's. She moves with a casual grace, whether standing or sitting, whether lighting a cigarette or gesturing to punctuate a thought.

"When I was sixteen I lived in a small community called South Beloit, Illinois, right outside of Wisconsin. I was in my junior year of high school, and I guess I spent most of my time dreaming about what it would be like to be seventeen. I had just read a book called *Seventeenth Summer,* and I imagined seventeen would be the magic year, a very romantic time. Most of my girlfriends felt the same way.

"I was involved in just about every extracurricular activity I could find. I guess I might have been a better scholar if I hadn't been, but study wasn't my primary interest. That year I was vice-president of my class, and I was a cheerleader—that was the big thing, cheerleading. I had it all planned that by my senior year I would become head of the cheerleaders. Really, I don't know how I did it all. I would devote every afternoon to some activity or club and come home for supper and rush back for more. It was very important to me to be involved in all these things.

"I had relatives in Chicago at that time, and I would visit there every summer and some weekends during the school year. Now this presented a conflict because my Chicago friends were what I thought of as urban and sophisticated, while I was still very much a country girl. It wasn't that I hadn't been exposed to things like movies and the theater, but I lived in a little town and went to a little high school and what I thought of as fun had nothing to do with what my Chicago friends thought was fun. It really was a problem, because a part of me had always wanted to be what I thought of as a city girl.

"My godmother was in many ways the image of what I wanted to be. Her name was Gloria (I was named after her), but everyone called her Go-go. She was only about fifteen years older than I, and I really think she must have been a sort of Auntie Mame to me. I tried in every way to be just like her. I used to wear her clothes and feel *so* fashionable and glamorous. I was a big girl, even at fourteen, and she would pass along some of her things to me, although she was always careful not to saddle me with anything too mature for my age. Mostly suits, I would wear her suits and feel like the epitome of glamor in them, except usually I would end up taking off the jacket. It was a skirt and sweater and saddle-shoe town, and I'd get sort of self-conscious after a while. There I was, a small-town girl yearning to be like my godmother and my Chicago friends."

A swift laugh and then a sudden second thought: "One of the most important things that happened when I was sixteen sounds pretty funny when I tell it, but I really think it had long-reaching effects. I played hooky from school for the first time. I had never done it before and I've never done it since, and I did it for no reason. Some of the senior girls decided to play hooky and they asked me if I wanted to join them. This was something special, because I was hardly ever absent, and no one had ever dared to ask me to play hooky. I thought about it for a while. It seemed sort of like the idea of smoking. I used to sneak a cigarette now and then, not because I had any need or liking for cigarettes, but because the senior girls were doing it. It was one of those things you do just because you're not supposed to.

"I decided I'd go ahead and play hooky. All we did was sit around at one of the girls' houses smoking cigarettes and talking about boys. Nothing would have happened except that I'd forgotten all about an assignment I was supposed to hand in for the school newspaper. They called my home to ask if they could come pick it up—naturally they thought I was sick—and my grandparents were absolutely stunned.

"When I came home, it was the most humiliating experience of my life. I was raised by my grandparents and they never laid a hand on me, never spanked me or disciplined me that way, but some things are worse than being hit. They literally couldn't understand why I had played hooky, and they called a family conference, actually called people in from Chicago to discuss it. They called my godmother, of course, and they called my great-uncle, a man called 'Gentleman Jim' who I thought was the most magnificent man in the world. He represented what a man in our family could be—a very educated person, what you would truly call a 'grand old man.' There was also another uncle from Chicago and one of my aunts from Beloit and my grandparents themselves, all the people I loved and respected most in the world, people I couldn't bear to disappoint.

"In the meantime my grandmother had also discovered a cigarette butt in the lining of my peajacket. She was getting ready to send it to the cleaners and found it by accident. So there I was, a girl who had played hooky and come home with cigarette butts in her jacket, waiting for all my relatives to arrive and hold a conference. I was too embarrassed to cry. I had absolutely no explanation to give. I wasn't a nervous girl, or a disturbed one. They couldn't say I was a fast girl because I don't think there were any girls in South Beloit who could be called fast. I had no excuse. I had just done it. My grandparents couldn't conceive of my having played hooky without a reason: they kept wondering what was troubling me. That was the worst part. I couldn't reassure them or explain it at all.

"I think I decided right then that I would never again in life do anything I couldn't defend myself on. Whether what I did was right or wrong, whether I might regret it later—that didn't make any difference. The important thing was to know my reasons at the moment I did any given thing, know them and feel they could be published on the front page of *The New York Times*. I really feel I made that decision at that precise moment, during the hooky conference when I was sixteen, and I believe I've tried to live my life accordingly. Not that I haven't done things I'm not very proud of, but I'd probably do these same things over again, given the same circumstances. They were defensible; I always had reasons for doing them which were clear-cut to me."

I said it seemed a remarkable decision for a sixteen-year-old girl to make, and Miss Foster replied that her grandparents were remarkable people. "If I was able to form opinions like that, it was due in part to their influence. They were always telling me that I was hard-headed or strong-willed, not rebellious, exactly, because I almost always went along with their wishes, but I let it be known that they weren't necessarily *my* wishes. I was never one to let things be done to me.

"My grandparents were very proud of me. It was important for me to maintain good grades because that mattered so much to them. I don't mean to make them sound self-righteous. They were real grandparents. I mean they were intelligent and loving but not super-sophisticated, modern types. I often think how wise they were to be so unschooled in their handling of me. Out of incidents like the family conference I formed ideas which permitted me to deal on a different level as I grew older.

"Well, that was the single most important incident in my sixteenth year. I went back to my whirl of cheerleading and writing for the school paper and Y-teens and what-have-you, and I kept making those visits to Chicago where I was painfully aware of how lacking I was in big-city know-how.

"I was very conscious of the fact that I had a good figure at the time, and I think I was pretty confident about my appearance. I was a healthy girl, and I had clear skin and fairly manageable hair. My braces had come off when I was about fifteen, so I had good teeth, too. All in all I couldn't complain about how I looked. What bothered me was the fact that my Chicago friends knew much more about boys than I did. They knew how to talk to them, what to say and how to react, and they all had boyfriends. I didn't have a boyfriend in Beloit at all, so my appearance became very important to me. I figured if I didn't have the other attributes I might as well look as good as they did, especially when I was sixteen.

"I had also lost my summer boyfriend. He was fifteen when I met him in Chicago and I was thirteen. He was a very brilliant young man; he was entering the University of Illinois at fifteen, which was really extraordinary. By the time of my sixteenth summer he had gone off with his college friends.

"In Beloit I didn't go out with boys because it was a small community, mainly Italian, and I was among the few Negroes who lived there. There was one Negro boy in my class, but he and I were just friends and didn't have any desire to date each other. We'd usually end up together at proms and such, but that was just because there was no one else. By my junior year, when everyone had started dating, I realized that I was left out of certain things. On Friday night, when we all went to get sodas, I was suddenly not with the most popular girls any more. They all had boyfriends. Even though I was one of the most popular girls during the regular school week, the separation would inevitably occur when it came time for dances and parties where the kids paired off.

"I was seldom aware of any discrimination or prejudice, but it was a little frustrating to have to console myself with the thought of my summer romance in Chicago. I just joined more activities. Whatever was missing in one area was always compensated for in another. I made sure of that."

I asked Miss Foster if she ever had to contend with well-meaning classmates who wondered why she and the Negro boy she had mentioned didn't fall in love.

"Oh, sure, of course," she replied. "That was a little puzzling to me. Why should we?

"I became especially proud of my figure at that time, because our social life revolved around going to the beach in Chicago, and I was proud to be looked at. I may not have been able to deal with things as grandly as my urban friends, but I got looked at all the same. I had a bright orange bathing suit, and I mean really bright. I still have it, even though I'd never wear it today. I came across it not long ago, and I just couldn't throw it away. It's the kind of bathing suit only a sixteen-year-old would wear. I remember vividly going to buy that suit and coming home and trying it on for my godmother. I was a very shapely girl and full-grown, and she just looked at me, standing there in her living room modeling that incredible thing, and kept shaking her head. Finally she said, 'It's a sin for you to look that way at sixteen, and you really shouldn't be allowed to wear it, but go ahead!' So I was allowed to wear my screaming orange bathing suit and show off on the beach all summer.

"I also remember I was very embarrassed because I had fallen arches. I used to practice ways of burying my feet in the sand so nobody would notice. I would work out these elaborate positions and experiment for hours holding my feet at certain angles to make it look as if I had an arch."

Miss Foster caught me glancing curiously at her most normal-looking feet and giggled. "You can't see them," she said, "that's the whole point. Nobody would have noticed them at all, but I thought they were perfectly glaring. That's another example of what my grandparents called my hard-headedness. I was supposed to wear these arch-support shoes when I was about fourteen, but they were so ugly I couldn't stand them. I never wore them, and if I had, I might have been better off. I'm sure if I could have ripped the braces off my teeth, I would have done that, too, but luckily I couldn't. Well, anyway, my sixteenth summer went by. I cavorted in my orange bathing suit and hid my feet in the sand, and one other thing happened. I began to think a little about the future, about what I might want to do after I graduated.

"In a town like South Beloit the extent of most girls' ambitions ended with marrying the boy they'd gone steady with and settling down directly after high school in South Beloit. Very rarely did you ever find anyone who was encouraged to pursue education beyond high school, in spite of the fact that Beloit College was right there. I was one of the few who were encouraged. Somehow my teachers got to me, somehow it came to me that I had to get beyond South Beloit, Illinois. Few people in my family had been college-educated except for my godmother and my great-uncle, 'Gentleman Jim.' I myself hadn't been what you'd call a brilliant scholar, but I was an A student and I was fortunate enough to have teachers who urged me to think ahead. One in particular, an English teacher named Mrs. Gruhlke, seemed always to be encouraging me to seek information beyond what was necessary to complete a given work. She taught me how to read, in a way, how to be curious about reading.

"She was a very special teacher—everyone loved Mrs.

Gruhlke. She was new to the school when I was there, and I don't even know where she came from, but she had such a wealth of imagination, such an ability to prod you into reaching out further. She obviously had a background that was beyond what you usually find in a small town. Along with my grandparents and my godmother, she was the major influence in making me want to get beyond South Beloit.

"My godmother was already thinking in terms of Eastern colleges, which meant absolutely nothing to me. When I think about it, it seems rather incredible, since we were hardly people of means. Also, it wasn't the sort of situation you'd find in a city, where everything is geared to a concept of higher education. I sometimes wonder, why me, of all the girls in that town? I think it was a combination of things: my grandparents' ability to think of me in terms beyond the immediate situation, and my own will to do something. There was something else— not loneliness, exactly, because I kept too busy and had too many friends to be too lonely—but a feeling I had of the limitations in my existence in high school. Before that, when I was very small, there had been even more limitations. I guess I haven't really described what a country girl I was.

"When my brother and I were young children, we lived on a farm in Janesville, Wisconsin. My grandparents had decided that the city wasn't a proper place for kids to be raised, and at their age, having already raised a set of kids, they pulled up their roots and took us to a little farm in Wisconsin so we could grow up in a healthy country atmosphere. It was a real farm, with cows and chickens and pigs, and nobody for miles around. My brother and I walked four miles to and from school every day, and there was no one to play with except our dog named Rover. I thought it was the loneliest place in the world.

"I had chores to do, like any farm kid (I managed to avoid

them a lot of the time), and once the chores were done I found myself reading and playing with paper dolls. Those were my two main activities. My godmother had enrolled me in a children's book club, and I would receive two or three books a month. I just couldn't get enough of those books: Zane Grey westerns and Nancy Drew mysteries and *The Black Stallion* and oh, my goodness, they were just the high point of life. And paper dolls! I would sit by the riverbank and play with paper dolls—movie-star paper dolls—Hedy Lamarr one day and Dorothy Lamour the next. I'm sure I played with paper dolls long beyond the time when most girls do, but for me they were companions. I even wrote stories for them from the books I had read. One was a motorcycle mystery. Can you imagine? I knew nothing about motorcycles, had never been on one, but I wrote the story just the same.

"It was a very lonely life in many ways, and undoubtedly that had a lot to do with the sort of person I became. Surely, part of the reason I threw myself into all those school activities when we moved to Beloit stemmed from loneliness. I developed a thirst for activity that probably accounted for a part of my drive to continue on with school. I didn't know what it was I wanted to be. I realized dimly, too, that it was not so much a matter of what I wanted as what was available to me. I surely had no intentions of becoming an actress. We didn't even have a drama club at our school. I used to imagine being a lawyer sometimes, but that was all very romantic. I thought of Portia's speech from *The Merchant of Venice* and I envisioned myself as a great criminal lawyer. I'm sure if anyone had sat me down in front of a book about contracts and torts, my enthusiasm would have dampened immediately.

"I had no heroes and heroines I wanted to pattern myself after. Except for my grandparents and my godmother and my great-uncle, there was nobody to emulate. I didn't even have movie-star heroes the way most girls do. When I dreamed of an ideal young man, for instance, I dreamed of a Negro. Now I could go to the movies for a month of Sundays and not find a Negro movie star to fantasize about. My family wasn't prejudiced, either, because there are some mixed marriages among us, but I personally always envisioned my perfect man as a Negro, a man of color. I was delighted to know that somewhere out there was a Lena Horne and a Marian Anderson, but as far as being inspired to do something by any public figure—no. And, strangely, I still don't have any heroes.

"During my senior year I began to take scholarship examinations, and I surprised myself by passing a number of them, even one to an Eastern college. The trouble was that even with the financial aid a scholarship would have given me, the expenses were unbelievable and there was no way to guarantee that I'd find work once I got there. I rejected the idea of the University of Chicago, even though my godmother had gone there, because I had so many relatives in Chicago and I didn't want to have to live with them. I wanted to be on my own.

"I finally wound up going to Illinois Normal, a state teachers college near Bloomington. That didn't necessarily mean I wanted to become a teacher, but it didn't seem a bad way to start out. Eventually I became completely bored with the curriculum there. It all seemed like busywork to me. The only things that kept me in school were the Debating and Oratory Societies, which I loved. By my second year I had won almost all the prizes in oratory and realized I was in school for all the wrong reasons. Once you'd won all the awards in the only area you cared about, what was left? I wasn't interested in acting then, even though there was a theater on campus. In fact we were rival forces. The debating people looked down on the theater people because they just mouthed what others had written for them. We, on the other hand, felt original and glorious!

"Once there were no further fields to conquer in debating I became very disillusioned, but I had left home to go to school and therefore it seemed very important to finish, so important that I got married at nineteen and left with my husband to live in Chicago. I enrolled in a teachers college there. Also, my husband and his whole family were well-educated, with lots of degrees among them, and I was becoming very much a part of the urban middle-class intellectual atmosphere. I managed to stick out two more semesters of teachers college before I realized I didn't want to teach, would never teach and was wasting my time. I said no, no more, I quit."

She made a dramatic gesture which showed how strongly she had felt, and drew a deep breath. "Then I just sort of stumbled on the Goodman Theater School. I can't even recall why I went there. I knew nothing about drama schools; all I knew was that the Goodman School had to do with working with the voice and with theater people. It seems silly now to say that I just dropped in, but that was how it happened. I asked them, 'What do you do here?' and they let me sit in on a voice and diction class. I was asked to read a piece of poetry— it was something by Edna St. Vincent Millay—and I did. The teacher was very impressed and the students were, too. That did it. I still didn't know I wanted to be an actress, as such, but I knew I found an exhilaration in reading that poem, and I knew it was an area of communication I wanted to be a part of, so I enrolled at Goodman.

"My husband's friends were very indulgent about my going to drama school. They were a good deal older than I was, and the whole thing was treated like a whim of mine—something one didn't take seriously. But I took it seriously. I began to take improvisation with Bella Itkin, along with the voice and diction and body work classes. This sort of discipline was totally new to me. Perhaps I shouldn't say discipline, because the whole point of improvisation is to bring something *out* of you. At first it's almost frightening. You know that your instructor is going to see you in weak moments, moments when you feel terribly insecure, and you know you must permit the teacher to assume that position if you're ever going to learn anything from her. Bella and I had some pretty rough days together. She used to say, 'Oh, quit thinking so much, Gloria, and just do it!' When things were going badly I could always tell because Bella would grab great handfuls of her hair and pull. It's a wonder she has a hair left on her head. But the good days! She didn't give praise easily, and one of her little slanted smiles and a comment like 'Good, Gloria,' was like a bouquet of roses. It was enough to lift my spirits for days.

"Bella was very rigid and very demanding with her students, and particularly with me, I think, because I became involved in some of the major projects at school. This put a lot of responsibility on my shoulders. I was carrying some major roles in plays and some of them were too old for me, like Medea. But it was a stretching school, and you were expected to go beyond what you thought were your own limitations.

"Bella directed me in most of these projects and some days she had me climbing the walls but I think it made things a little easier for me once I began to work in the professional theater. I don't think I suffered any feelings of resentment when a director told me what to do. I've noticed a lot of New York actors seem to be embarrassed or insulted when they have to be told something. It hurts, of course, but you can't let it get in your way. You can't see yourself, and you need your energy to concentrate on the character you create. If you don't believe in your director, you're not going to believe in yourself.

"The director guides you and uses your resources, but you, the actor, must feel free to do the most outlandish things in order to arrive at the right thing. That's what we have the most trouble bringing out of ourselves: the freedom to experiment with approaches that might be terribly wrong. It's like the business of me playing Medea at the Goodman School at nineteen. Of course it stretched me, of course I was too young, but it kept me wanting. It gave me a taste of what could be done."

Had she ever thought then about the odds against success in the theater? I asked. Or felt that being a Negro might make it particularly difficult?

"When I first started out," she replied, "I don't honestly think I ever felt that being a Negro would be an obstacle in the theater. I've always been very aware of being a Negro, and intensely proud, back in the days when I was the only Negro girl in South Beloit, as much as now. I felt then that there were things expected of me which were not expected of the other girls. I knew I was different, of course, and knew it most keenly when the business of dating arose, and I had no date and daydreamed about Negro boyfriends in Chicago. But I never felt handicapped by the difference. In Chicago when I was first married I would sometimes go to apply for jobs and later people would say, 'But, Gloria, Negroes never apply for jobs at such-and-such a place.' I was always amazed, because I was so unaware of these things. If I saw a job and it looked interesting to me, I'd go investigate it.

"It was the same when I realized that theater would be my career: I never thought in terms of being limited because of my color. But I do now. Now I realize there can be very real limitations; there is a tendency to cast the Negro as a Negro, as I was in *In White America*. But other roles should be open, too. One great function of the theater is to use creativity and imagination to take dramatic advantage of all the differences available in actors, of different skin colors and hair textures. Certainly if Negroes are confined to roles in plays about civil rights or the South, they will have no opportunity to exercise themselves fully as actors. It's an important issue, and no matter how unaware of it I was when I started, I'm certainly not un-aware of it now."

Did she have any advice for aspiring actresses?

"I can't say how strongly I feel about good training," she replied. "I get letters all the time from kids who tell me they're in their last year of high school and they know they're ready for the professional theater. They don't want to waste any more time, they say. Think of it. All I can tell them is, for heaven's sake stay in school. These kids have no conception of what the professional theater is like, and they haven't been trained. An actor has only himself, a self-contained unit, and what are you in terms of acting but a body and a voice, emotions and experiences? If you haven't learned how to use that body, that voice, to express your emotions and experiences, you're not going to last very long.

"Another thing—even in the acting schools like Goodman, which take care to train you rigorously, the students don't really understand what it's going to be like in the professional theater. You're used to thinking in terms of the theater being an acting assignment. But when you leave school you realize that first of all there has to be a job available for you. You aren't simply handed a role, as you are in school. You must build up a reputation in order to be considered for an impor-tant part. There are directors and producers and public taste and critics to please, and it's all totally different from anything you imagine when you're attending school. In the New York theater community you sometimes have three weeks to get a show together and suddenly you find yourself performing in front of a preview audience after that ridiculously short rehearsal period. It's not at all like the idealistic atmosphere of the drama school, and I think it ought to be the function of these schools to somehow prepare students for life in the real theater world. There ought to be a way of explaining that performing for a paying audience is not the same as getting up in front of your friends and your acting coach.

"I hear actors speaking all the time of the plans they've made for launching their careers. Plans are fine, of course, but how can you plan in a business as unpredictable as theater? When I came to New York it wasn't the result of planning at all. I had visited a friend in New York the year before, and we all ended up at an agent's house reading from *A Raisin in the Sun*. It was purely a social occasion; we were just reading for the fun of it. But a year later when a tour of that play was sent out, the agent remembered me and sent word to Chicago that he'd like me to appear in it. I had to think it over, of course, because it meant leaving life as I had known it and involved a lot of personal decisions. But I went, and I never regretted it. I had stayed in school training myself to become an actress people would remember and want to use. That's why the producer chose me, that and luck. If I had read for him in a formal audition atmosphere instead of at a party where we were all relaxed, who knows? It's all so unpredictable.

"Later, when I came out of a fourteen-month run of *In White America*, I was lucky enough to go into *Medea* because a producer, Judy Mareschal, believed I should do the role. Now I'm afraid I'm being typed as a strictly classical actress. I would love to do a naturalistic play or a comedy for a change of pace."

Miss Foster excused herself for a moment. When she reappeared, she was dressed in stark black, an ankle-length skirt over a leotard. We left the dressing room and walked down the hall together. From many doors along the way people called hello.

I asked Miss Foster about the film she planned to do with Richard Burton in Africa.

"I'm leaving in two weeks, as soon as *Yerma* closes," she said. "First I have to be tutored in a Haitian-French accent. I start lessons tonight. It's a small but very good part and, just think, it'll be my first trip out of the country—and Africa at that." Her young smile flashed out. "Isn't that terrific?" she said.

Marisa Berenson

She was called "Girl of the Year" in 1966 by New York fashion editor Eugenia Sheppard. Her lineage is distinguished: she is the granddaughter of the famous French couturière and parfumière Elsa Schiaparelli and the grandniece of the art historian Bernard Berenson, renowned for his studies of Italian Renaissance painting.

Though not yet twenty-one, she is well on her way to achieving fame, too. One of America's leading high-fashion models, she has been photographed for the covers and pages of Vogue, Bazaar, Life *and other publications, and has appeared in numerous television commercials. "Many faces are beautiful and alluring, but hers is chic," says Diana Vreeland, editor of* Vogue. *Other observers see in her smile a Mona Lisa quality that is intriguing and mysterious.*

Born February 15, 1947, she is the oldest daughter of Robert Berenson and Maria-Luisa Yvonne Schiaparelli. Her father's work, first as a shipping line executive and then as an American government official in Yugoslavia and a foreign service officer, gave her and her sister Berinthia a chance to see a good deal of the world. At vacation time they traveled from their schools to wherever their parents were living at the moment.

She studied in England, Italy and Switzerland, at schools that are known for being "exclusive," and continues to live her life in fashionable surroundings. She was probably the youngest guest at Truman Capote's famous masked ball at New York's Plaza Hotel, and she travels frequently from New York to London and Paris, as well as to more distant parts of the world on modeling assignments.

Marisa Berenson

RED VINYL DRAPES cover one wall of Marisa Berenson's living room; in the foyer, zebra-striped wallpaper runs over doors, ceiling and walls. A tiny Pekinese dog squeaked at her heels as she let me in, then ran crazy circles of excitement around the room. "That's enough," she said. "Now you're going to be banished." She picked the dog up and carried it to the bedroom. Shutting the door, she came back smiling. It was a gentle smile, out of tune with the fashionable dog and the mod décor.

Marisa Berenson's face seems familiar. It has appeared, of course, in the pages of many magazines, but beyond that it seems familiar as a good painting seems familiar, even at first sight. There is a feeling of rightness, of a surprising and delightful perfection. Her eyes are large, heavily lashed and green. Like her smile, they reflect a delicate shyness.

She was dressed in well-tailored slacks and a tan cashmere sweater with a scarf knotted at her throat. Hardly the overly made-up, crazily dressed version of a model, she is simply a deliciously beautiful girl who happens to earn her living by posing before a camera.

"I was the most awful creature in the world at sixteen," she began, sitting cross-legged on a plaid-covered couch. "I was difficult and independent, I wanted my own way. I was in school in Florence, Italy, and I hated it. The school was called the Poggio Imperiale and it was run very strictly. When I was there, we had fifteen girls, all from different countries. We were taught languages—Italian, French, German and English —the history of art, the theater, literature—a very liberal kind of education and, I suppose, a pretty good one. But I still thought it was a hideous place. The school was in this ancient palazzo, dark and gloomy, with frescoes on the walls, not the kind of place that would appeal to a sixteen-year-old girl. And we had to wear uniforms: gray dresses, a cape, high white collars. We were never allowed out of the building except on Sundays.

"I really hated the whole idea of school. I wanted to be doing something on my own. I hated being pushed around the way they push you around in a school. I don't believe that true learning comes from having things drummed into you. When I had to take an exam, I went blank; pressure seemed to do that to me. Anyway, I don't believe in exams. Most people don't remember too many of the things they're forced to learn like that. You can learn a lot more from traveling, I think, from meeting people and living your own life in the fullest way. Learning should be a relaxed thing to be really effective, and this school kept such a close rein on us. My parents had lots of friends in Florence, but of course I couldn't see them very much because we could only go out on Sundays and we had to be back by eight o'clock at night. I suppose there's some reason for strict rules with a group of sixteen-year-old girls living in a strange city, but I didn't feel that way then. I just thought the whole thing was unfair. And several times I got into trouble because I didn't get in on time—once I stayed out until two in the morning and the teachers were frantic—and I broke other rules, too. The one effect all those rules had on me was to make me even more anxious to get away from school completely. I couldn't wait until I got out and could begin working."

Stretching back against the couch, she smoothed her hair from her face, which gave her a composed look that had nothing in common with adventurous rule-breaking. "Didn't you think of going to college?" I asked.

"Not really," she said. "You see, I had a European kind of upbringing and education, and for women in Europe going to college isn't too common unless you're really some kind of brain. I wasn't that academic in school. I've always been more interested in artistic things. I love art. I can speak four languages fairly well and I read a lot, but I was never a great student. The main thing was that I wanted to be on my own, to accomplish something by myself.

"I suppose that partly I was rebelling against my parents. I resented them telling me what to do. In a lot of ways I think I had a horrible character when I was that age. Now I think my parents are great and that they gave my sister and me an absolutely marvelous life. I adored them when I was sixteen, too, of course, but in a different way. *Then* I couldn't help feeling that they weren't on my side. There were so many things I wanted to do and I was so frustrated at not being able to do them." She uncrossed her long legs and tossed her head; her hair brushed across her face. Right at the moment it seemed that there were many things she wanted to be doing.

"Of course, I was away from home a lot as a child. From the time I was nine years old I was in boarding schools, first in

Switzerland, next in England for five years and then Florence. But that didn't really have anything to do with my being sort of a rebel. I think I would have been one even if I had stayed home to go to school. I hated the whole idea of school.

"But now I realize that it wasn't so bad for me to be kept down by my parents. In England at school, I knew girls whose parents either didn't know or didn't care what they were doing, and the results were disastrous. I mean they did ridiculous things, just ran wild at much too young an age. A lot of them got married too young and I think they're terribly sorry now. A young person does need someone to keep her under control. If I'd been allowed to do what I wanted when I was sixteen, I would have done silly things.

"One thing that pushed me away from school, now that I think about it, is that I was usually with older people. Even in school my friends were older than I was and when I went to parties or out with a boy, the boy was older, the people at the parties were older. I guess seeing the kind of life they were living, the things they were doing, rubbed off on me and I wanted to be like that, not having to obey teachers in school. That's my thing about not wanting to be pushed around. My sister is very different. She's sweet and divine and loved by all. She's very intelligent and she has a terrific personality. She always worked very hard at whatever she was doing and somehow she didn't seem to mind the"—she hesitated—"well, I guess the word is 'system.' She just went along with things the way they were. When I used to try and influence her, my mother would say: 'Stop ruining your sister's life. She grew up normally. You were never a child.'

"Of course I don't think it's true that I was never a child; I was just different from my sister and I wanted to do things that my mother didn't think I was ready for. My sister took things in stride and I couldn't. Maybe I had a complex about her because she did better than I did, in school, for instance. She was always very good in class."

What she had said about her sister, I suggested, made her sound less self-assured than she seemed to be. She giggled at me: "Oh, of course I'm a little insecure. I have qualms about being accepted. Actually, I'm frightfully shy. But when I get out in a group of people, at a party, for instance, I like being the center of attention, I like meeting people, I like to dance. I don't like to sit in a corner, out of things, just looking on. Maybe the fact that I like to jump around, to talk and giggle, is one way of hiding the insecurity. If you have certain things going for you, then you live with this—the insecurity, if that's what it is. I mean, you just try to do what you think you should do. I'm very excited about acting, for instance, but I'm also insecure about it. I have to be told all the time that I'm good. If I go to see someone about a part, I'm nervous. I need a lot of reassurance, but that doesn't stop me from trying. I don't know if I'll make it, but I have to try."

I asked why she wanted to give up modeling in favor of acting when her modeling career was going so well.

"I always wanted to be a model. When I was young, I kept scrapbooks and pasted pictures from magazines into them. So modeling was very exciting for me at first. And I was working with the best photographers in the world and being photographed in all those marvelous clothes. What girl wouldn't like that? But after a while modeling can get tiresome, it can get on your nerves. Now I have the feeling that I'm not accomplishing that much. Of course, the traveling is still great fun, but modeling doesn't seem as stimulating as it used to be. I get an enormous thrill now out of the thought of being an actress. That seems like a terrific challenge, to be a good actress. Of course, I don't know if I have the talent, but I am studying—at Philip Burton's school, the American Music and Dramatic Academy."

Again she brushed her hair away from her cheek and bounced forward excitedly on the couch. "Acting just seems much more worthwhile to me. To be a good actress requires a certain amount of intelligence, and the use of it in what you are doing. It's probably connected with liking to be the center of attention, too, being involved instead of just looking on.

"Even when I was sixteen, I felt this way. I felt that the big thing in life was to achieve something. I probably matured a lot faster than many girls do because of the way our family has lived. I think the same thing is true of my sister. She finished school when she was seventeen, too. Now she's working as a photographer in London, and she's quite good at it. There's a sort of independence we have that many girls don't feel until they're older.

"I think it's because our family traveled around so much. Since Father was in the foreign service, he had posts in a lot of different countries. My sister and I were away at boarding school most of the year, but during vacations we went to wherever my father and mother were. So we got to spend two or three months in a lot of different countries. I feel that we both learned a lot from traveling, and from our parents. They were the kind of people who had an enormous number of friends who adored them, and they had a great life. They liked knowing how to live in a marvelous way.

"Most young people don't have the opportunity to travel very much, and I think you can learn as much traveling as you can in school, maybe more. When you go to a foreign country, you just naturally see things you wouldn't see at home, and you're thrown in with kinds of people you wouldn't meet at home. We saw all sides of life in foreign countries. When I was fourteen, for example, I traveled through Libya. It was fascinating—all that desert—totally different from anything I'd ever seen before." She emphasized the point with a wave of her hand.

She was wearing five rings, mostly jade and gold bands, on her hand. They reminded me of a fashion photograph, and I asked: "How did you get started as a model?"

"It just happened," she said. "After the school in Florence, I went to another school in London, kind of a finishing school, sort of covering all the angles." She giggled at the memory. "We learned typing and shorthand and things like that, so we could go right out and get a job. But we were also taught to cook and other domestic things, preparation for marriage, you know. Anyway, I went to London and started to work as an interior decorator. I didn't love that too much and I decided to try modeling. Then my father became ill and I came to America to be with him. Mrs. Vreeland, the editor of *Vogue*, who is an old friend of my parents, asked me to do some test shots. The magazine liked them, and suddenly I was on the cover. After that, I was sort of launched." She smiled brightly and again her hand went to her cheek. The movement drew attention to her face, as did many of her gestures. Was this a carryover from the hours in front of a camera?

"On my first modeling job," she continued, "I wasn't very sure of myself. I was self-conscious, in fact, but of course you learn. Modeling isn't as easy as some people think it is. It's terribly glamorous but also terribly tough work. Most days you go from eight in the morning to six at night. When you get to a photographer's studio, you may have to sit around for quite a while; then you may have to do fifty shots in two hours. And of course you always have to look right. That often means putting on makeup in ten minutes, which isn't so easy. Some days you may have sittings at five different studios, so you'll be running around town like crazy. And when the photographer is working with you, you don't just stand there. You have to concentrate on the feeling he's trying to get, you have to produce the expressions he wants. Actually, what you do in front of the camera is quite a bit like acting.

"Location trips are different, of course. Sometimes they're a lot of fun because you're with nice people in a place you haven't been before, but mostly they're very hectic and nerve-racking. Most of the photographers are very easy to work with, but there are some who are difficult—one, I absolutely loathe. Still, it's marvelous to be traveling. I've been on location in Jamaica, Antigua, Spain, California and Mauritius, a marvelous island in the Indian Ocean."

"Hasn't all this traveling made you want to live in some faraway place that you've seen?" I asked.

"No," she said, "not really. The two places I like the best are New York and Paris. They're quite different from each other but I like them both. New York seems very fast to me, very modern and international, full of excitement. And New York is very free. In New York it doesn't matter who your family is or where you came from. What matters is whether or not you've made something out of yourself. In Paris, it's much more snobby, at least for me. I have friends there that I've known all my life and there is a great awareness of class. You have to more or less stay with people from your own class, your own background. Paris seems to me to be very calm compared to New York. There are night clubs, of course, but not like in New York, and everyone goes to the same ones—New Jimmy's or Castel's. There's nothing in Paris as wild as Cheetah or some of the other New York places. But of course Paris is really my home. My grandmother has a marvelous house there, and my parents and my sister and I live on the top floor. A very old house, with a garden and a courtyard, and it's filled with paintings and elegant old furniture and objects. It's really quite a marvelous house. I'm leaving for Paris in a few days, as a matter of fact, and I'll be glad to get back to it."

I remarked on her look of excitement, which seems to be characteristic. She smiled in response. "Well, I like what I'm doing," she said. "It seems to me that it's much freer for a girl now than it was when I was young. Now a girl can do what she wants. Ten years ago, it wasn't nearly as easy. Ultimately, what I'd like to have is a home, a husband and children, a full and healthy life. When I'm married, though, I intend to do something; I'm not going to sit home and twiddle my thumbs. But I don't think very much about the future. One thing I've learned since I was sixteen is that it's very bad to want everything to happen right away. When I was sixteen, I couldn't wait for anything. Now I'm very happy to be able to desire something, work for it, and hope it will come to be."

Mary S. Calderone, M.D.

Mary Steichen Calderone was born on July 1, 1904, to the photographer Edward J. Steichen and his wife Clara. As the daughter of a brilliant artist, she grew up in a home that encouraged creativity and original thinking. Her parents were divorced when Mary was a child, and she and her sister Kate were separated, Mary living with friends, and Kate with their mother. From then on, her life was subject to frequent change, as she went to live with first one friend of her father's and then another. A lonely, serious child, she was much more at home listening to the conversation of adults than playing with other children. Indeed, her playthings were ideas, exchanged across the dinner table among the artists her father knew.

She attended Brearley, a private girls' school in New York City, then went to Vassar College, graduating in 1925 at twenty-one. She spent the next three years with the American Laboratory Theater. During this period, she married and her daughter, Linda, was born. In 1928 she collaborated with her photographer father to create the best-selling First and Second Picture Book—*the first time photographs had been used successfully in books for children.*

When her marriage ended in divorce, she turned to the study of medicine. She received her M.D. from the University of Rochester Medical School in 1939, and her M.A. from Columbia University School of Public Health. After an internship of one year with the Children's Medical Service of Bellevue Hospital, her concern shifted from the actual practice of medicine to public health and preventive medicine. In 1953 she became Medical Director of the Planned Parenthood Federation of America, a post she held for eleven years.

She married, in 1941, Dr. Frank A. Calderone, who shaped his wife's interest in public health. A former Deputy Commissioner of Health of New York City, he has also served with the World Health Organization and with the United Nations Secretariat. They have two daughters, Francesca and Maria, and two teenage grandsons. All share a common hobby, sailing, and the family has logged hundreds of miles of blue sea in their schooner, Tradition.

Mary S. Calderone, M.D.

In 1964 Dr. Calderone resigned from Planned Parenthood to help found and direct a voluntary health agency, Sex Information and Education Council of the United States, Inc. Known as SIECUS, its purpose is "to establish man's sexuality as a health entity." With respect to young people in particular, Dr. Calderone and SIECUS are urging the nation's schools to institute more and broader classes in education for healthy and responsible sexuality.

Mary S. Calderone, M.D.

Dr. CALDERONE has gentian-blue eyes and classic, sculptured cheekbones. At the age of sixty-two she is a beautiful woman, and a busy one. I felt privileged to be admitted to her office at the Sex Information and Education Council of the United States (SIECUS), but Dr. Calderone was quite relaxed. She seemed delighted to see me, and when she spoke, her voice was so startlingly rich that I asked her about it. "I acted with the American Laboratory Theater for three years before I returned to medicine," she said. "But that's getting a little ahead of myself. I'd like to discuss the present just for a moment, if you don't mind. I'm very pleased with things today.

"I've just accepted invitations to go to some boys' schools, Groton and St. Paul's, to talk about what we're trying to accomplish here at SIECUS. I can't tell you how strongly I feel that we've short-changed our American boys on sex education. Sex education is a long process which begins in babyhood and continues throughout life. Relationships between men and women are not just in-bed relationships. A sexual relationship occurs every time a man and a woman meet, or for that matter, every time a man and man meet, or a woman and another woman. Does that sound surprising? Well, let me explain.

"You see, I don't regard sex merely as a matter of genital organs or genital acts. It is much larger than that. But our society doesn't see it that way. Society has slanted practically all its efforts on behalf of girls to seeing that they don't become pregnant. That's apparently all we care about, unfortunately, and so psychosexual maturation as a human being in boys *and* girls is usually completely ignored. We need to help everyone understand that sexuality is a part of the total personality, that it is the sum of all that you are as a man or a woman. Therefore I think it's a great pity that women are so overeducated in the subtleties that go into making a relationship, and boys get none of it. I'm very concerned about this, and no discussion on myself or anyone else at sixteen would be complete without my having said it. There, I've said my piece. Now, what would you like to know about me?"

I asked Dr. Calderone to tell me about herself at sixteen.

"I was, like so many young people, a mixture of confidence and insecurity. From the very first, I knew that my father loved me and expected great things of me. I wanted to merit his confidence in me, and somehow there was never any doubt in my mind that I would *be* something. In that respect, I was a very confident girl, not overbearingly so, just sure of myself.

"What insecurities I had arose from the fact that my mother had removed herself from me at a very early age—my parents were separated—and I had no real home. I was sort of farmed out, and even though it was to loving friends, it made me very insecure emotionally. And I was very lonely, too, but I never doubted that someday I would find what I wanted to do and do it. That really seemed quite clear-cut to me.

"In many ways I don't remember feeling very different at sixteen than I do now, or for that matter at three or four. I always had a well-defined sense of myself. Of course, I wasn't always happy, far from it, but I knew who I was. The fact that I went through two bouts of psychoanalysis, in my twenties and forties, shows that I was well aware of my failings and weaknesses. I was able to seek help, which is tremendously important.

"I'm sure that a great deal of my self-awareness came from having a father who approved of me thoroughly. My father, Edward Steichen, a great, great man, had such a sense of himself that he was able to leave school when he was fourteen and educate himself—one of the best-educated men of our times. I had him as an example, you see. You do know who he is, don't you?" [I nodded. Edward Steichen is one of America's most distinguished photographers, known to many for his *Family of Man* exhibit mounted when he was Director of Photography for the Museum of Modern Art in New York.]

"Well, then, you see how fortunate I was in having an influence like that. A man who gave himself an opportunity to test himself, find out who he was. It is much more difficult these days. Teenagers don't have the same freedom to branch out on their own this way. It is no longer possible to drop out of school at fourteen and feed your own mind.

"I went to the Brearley School here in New York City, which even in those days was one of the toughest schools in the country. In my junior year, when I was sixteen, I suddenly decided I'd had enough of school. They allowed me to take one extra course and take the rest of the examinations on my own. I did, and I got into Vassar College a year before I would have completed school. I wasn't really a Phi Beta Kappa student.

When I got to Vassar I had mostly B's and C's, but I was able, at that age, to make my own decisions, to *test* myself. Do you see what I mean?

"It's not so unusual as it may seem. My husband went to Columbia without having finished high school and, as I said, my father dropped out at fourteen. You could do that in those days. Now the competitive drive is so great that the colleges insist on high-school records. Kids aren't given the opportunity to strike out on their own, and I think that many of them would like to.

"How fortunate I was to grow up with intellectual stimulation always around me. When I was small I lived in France with my father, and men like Brancusi, the sculptor, were always dropping by to talk. One of my greatest pleasures was hearing these conversations and feeling a part of them. I also lived for a time in my early teens in the home of Dr. Leopold Stieglitz, brother of Alfred Stieglitz, the photographer, and I remember he would talk to me by the hour. At lunch he would tell me about his medical cases almost as if I were an adult. No matter where I went—I also lived with an aunt in Connecticut who was married to a modest, impecunious sculptor—there was always good talk. I learned to enjoy using my mind and participating in conversations with vigorous, productive people. To me, it was great fun.

"Part of the reason for my feeling of aloneness at the Brearley School was that I was completely different from the other girls. They were social, 'society,' and I was not. I was poor and didn't have the right clothes, so there was a great gap between me and my classmates. Not that I couldn't have fun— I adored parties—but my conception of pleasure was different from theirs and so I wasn't popular. I loved good conversation, listening to the viewpoints and concepts of stimulating people.

My classmates probably considered that a rather eccentric definition of fun.

"Besides my father, there were three great influences on my early life, three women. When I say great influences, I mean that my relationships with them affect me to this very day. One was my Aunt Charlotte, my mother's sister. She taught me the joy of physical work, doing it well. She was very poor but could make hard work a joyous thing because she had great spirit and integrity. She taught me to wash dishes and pick beans and make bread. We worked in her garden together and canned vegetables. We did things which could be considered drudgery, but she did them so beautifully and with such happiness that to this day I enjoy housework. If I am alone I will cook myself a superb meal and enjoy it all by myself, because I learned to love doing this from my aunt. She also had a tremendous impatience for dishonesty, toward oneself as well as others.

"Another important influence was a woman named Ann Dunn, a very great teacher at the Brearley School. She had faith in me. Like my father, she simply assumed that I would *be* something, and she taught me that I had obligations to whatever it was I chose to do. It wasn't a compulsive you-must-be-neat-and-you-must-work kind of thing. She instilled in me the feeling that I must live up to myself and develop work habits— what I call ideal-building.

"She was imaginative and, luckily for me, taught writing. With her help I was able to bring creativeness, which was a part of me naturally, into my writing. It had always been with me, but it was undisciplined. She didn't always pound at punctuation and grammar; she let me experiment with flair and creativity, but she didn't let me get away with anything messy either. Now I have an excellent approach to writing and editing, and I know she laid the groundwork for it by teaching me to have a sense of doing things well—the mechanics.

"She also gave me something else just as important, and that was love. She loved me dearly, as did my aunt and the others I have mentioned. It was always in terms of: 'I love you. I may not approve of what you're doing right now, but I love you.' Miss Dunn even bought me my graduation dress, because I had no money. I wouldn't have had a graduation dress at all if it hadn't been for her. That's the sort of person she was.

"The third great woman to change my life was Mrs. George Pratt, Helen Sherman Pratt, a very wealthy woman and a great philanthropist. She sort of took me under her wing, me, the daughter of a poor artist, and gave me the money which eventually sent me to college. She paid for music lessons when I took up piano, and I might have ended up playing professionally except I knew I wasn't good enough.

"The important thing is that all these people did things *with* me as well as *for* me. They enjoyed me as a person. I wasn't just a child, I was someone they enjoyed being with, and therefore I lived up to this and had the sense of giving back to them.

"Mrs. Pratt had me with her a great deal. She took me on trips and I would visit her in her home out in Glen Cove or in the summers in Maine. She was a very brilliant and gifted woman and way ahead of her time, a great believer in voluntary health organizations, a tremendous leader in many fields. She helped to start the Orchard Settlement House in Glen Cove, one of the first settlement houses for Negro people. She realized that here was a group with no facilities for recreation and education. This was way back in 1916—uncommon then.

"Mrs. Pratt had an enormous joy for living, like Miss Dunn and my aunt. Here they were, these three women, one very wealthy, one very poor and one a schoolteacher, yet they all shared one thing: to enjoy what you can do for someone else. My aunt received many favors from people—for example, Mrs. Pratt gave her husband orders for various kinds of sculptures— yet she never stopped giving to other people. When she died she had two sets of underwear in her drawer, two sets mended and mended, over and over again. So I've always had a sense of the obligation to give, of the idea that giving is a two-way street. These people, all of them tremendous givers, balanced out the grim, lonely side of me. I needed them.

"You must understand that, as the daughter of a poor artist, I was at school with girls who were totally unlike me. The school made generous tuition adjustments for me, but I was among very, very wealthy girls who could wear a fresh dress every day. I had to wear one dress all week long. Some of the more snobbish girls looked down on me for this, which made me feel uncomfortable, so the sense of difference was always there, naturally.

"Luckily, I wasn't too vain—perhaps the fact I had no clothes to fool around with helped me there—so I didn't worry about my appearance. I always wore hand-me-downs, and I didn't fret about it. I had a sense that I was beautiful, although my beauty was very different from the accepted style of beauty at the time. I would have been perfect for today. I had long, lank hair and high cheekbones, and that was in the days when Mary Miles Minter was considered the epitome of feminine beauty, you know, small features, pouting lips and tight curls everywhere.

"Even though I somehow knew myself to be beautiful, I also knew it wouldn't be very important to me unless I became beautiful inside. I didn't behave very beautifully a lot of the time, either. That was something I knew I had to fight against. I was very difficult to be with, sharp with people, apt to tell them what to do, driving and ambitious. I know a lot of my contemporaries found me arrogant and overbearing.

"I was even extremely nasty to some of the people I loved most dearly. I used to have knock-down, drag-out fights with my Aunt Charlotte. I would pit my will against hers, test myself, which I know now is a part of growing up. She was the only person I really had the luxury of testing myself against emotionally. I never did this with Mrs. Pratt because to me she was a magic person, and as far as Miss Dunn was concerned, she was a schoolteacher and one had too much respect for teachers to really fight with them. Other people I lived with I treated very badly. I loved them—don't misunderstand me— but I treated them badly. I was ruthless.

"I was always a great deal older than my real age. At sixteen I was like a twenty-one-year-old; at twenty-one I was twenty-six. I'm only just now catching up to my age. I look back with great regret on the fact that my Aunt Charlotte died without ever having known how I felt about her. It's only in the past ten or fifteen years that I've become aware of what she did for me. But there's no way to go back and make up for what you haven't done. You live with these things all your life—you can't ever make it up. I was just a terribly difficult girl.

"Oh, but sixteen was a marvelous, exciting time. I was intellectually mature and just going to college of my own volition. Of course I wasn't emotionally mature. In many ways I was still just a young girl, I even went through the ritual of putting up my hair and letting down my skirts on my sixteenth birthday. Literally. That may be hard to understand today, but it signified that I was ready to enter the world of coming out and going to parties. I'd been to parties, but in a different way. Now I was supposedly a young woman. But I remember how on my birthday I washed my hair and had a hot-iron Marcel wave and put it up and all the hairpins kept falling out."

Had Dr. Calderone found the ritual foolish, since she felt herself more mature than her friends? "Oh, no!" As if I had suggested something dreadful, her blue eyes widened. "Don't misunderstand me. I was a normal, romantic girl with as many daydreams as the next. I enjoyed it immensely, becoming sixteen, and I was very excited. My mother sent me my grandmother's little diamond ring—my oldest daughter has it today. These things had meaning then.

"Yes, it sometimes seems to me that our young people of today have been gypped of their rituals. A ritual which has some limits to it gives you a comfortable benchmark against which to measure your status. It lets you know a little bit more about who you are. One of the things I feel most strongly about is the way we have kept young people out of any meaningful participation in running society. We ghettoize them, push them into a corner with their Beatles and phonograph records and funny clothes, and say, 'Don't bother us until you're ready to come out and earn your living.' I feel absolutely violent about this. To imply that teenagers are of no use to us is devastatingly wrong. We need them terribly. In all our Headstart and early education programs we need them desperately.

"Our forefathers learned to grow up by watching their parents go through long and sometimes difficult periods of child rearing. And what do we do? We simply relegate our children to passive activities like baby-sitting, nothing that can truly fill the need for emotional participation. Take even the term 'baby-sitting'—it's a far cry from baby-nurturing.

"I wasn't lucky enough to have this kind of participation as a child, either—my younger sister lived with my mother, and we were estranged until we were grown up—but that doesn't mean I can't recognize the tremendous importance of it.

Everyone grows up basically alone now. There is no real community life any more. In my day we still had patterns, for better or worse.

"I had one really good friend named Ethel at Brearley, a wonderful girl. Although I don't see her often, I know she's still wonderful today in spite of great tragedy in her life—warm and loving and intelligent without being bookish. I was bookish, and I needed a friend of that sort. She was a friend in the real sense of the word. It must not have been easy, I told you how difficult I was. She, too, helped to balance me. I needed gentler influences to bring me out of myself.

"Of course we thought about boys constantly, but in those days you couldn't really have dates with boys. You met them at tea dances. They all came down from their schools, and we met under the clock at the Biltmore Hotel. How all of Yale, Harvard, Vassar, Brearley and all the other schools and colleges could meet under that one clock I'll never know, but we managed. Then we'd go tea-dancing, which meant quite literally that you went somewhere like the Plaza and drank tea and danced. There were several big parties over the holidays, and usually a cousin of Ethel's would escort me and we'd all go together."

There was rarely any single dating then until you met the boy you became engaged to or met someone you actually could feel serious about. It was more like the Swedish pattern today in which you do things in groups until you're about seventeen and then branch out into single dating which may lead to marriage. When I was sixteen, you didn't have a young man for a friend—he was an escort, really. All the same, I thought of nothing but boys when I was sixteen, I can assure you of that. I always thought in terms of the boys I knew and what was wrong with them, and the man I would eventually marry, who would be, of course, perfect. I always had strong sexual feelings, too.

"At twenty-one I married someone I thought was that man, the one I had fantasies about, and it didn't work out. I was divorced in five years with two children. *Of course* it didn't work out: I had invested this man with all sorts of imaginary qualities and tried to force him into an image. The qualities with which I had endowed him were purely egocentric: he would be for me all the things *I* needed—father, husband, lover—it was all in terms of what he would do for *me*. Naturally I thought of giving to him, too, but that was just as egocentric. I thought of sort of conferring on him this brilliant"—Dr. Calderone smiled—"witty, beautiful"—she burst into laughter—"female! He was supposed to be just so grateful.

"You see how immature I was even after college. I hadn't grown up in a home of my own, and nothing had ever prepared me for marriage itself. I had read all the standard novels: Thomas Hardy and Thackeray and the moderns like Scott Fitzgerald, but no studies of marriage which might have helped me to understand. All my visions of marriage at sixteen were completely selfish. I could think only of what *I* needed.

"What a romantic I was at sixteen! I still am. I liked very much the poetry of Vachel Lindsay. I also liked Sandburg because he had married my father's sister, but I didn't understand his poetry too well. Vachel Lindsay's poetry didn't make too many intellectual demands but it was so exciting. I heard him read 'The Congo,' and he was a very dramatic reader. He made you see things so clearly, it was wonderful. I *saw* the Congo and the jungles. I began to write some poetry myself, and of course I thought it was most wonderful. At the same time, though, I knew I could never be a really great poet. As soon as I realized that about anything I lost interest. If I couldn't be the best at something, I didn't really want to involve myself any more.

"I thought *Kristin Lavransdatter* by Sigrid Undset was the best novel ever written, and I read it three times. I still think it's a great book. In many ways it was autobiographical and I simply read myself into it. Even though Kristin was of the fifteenth century and I of the twentieth, I identified with her greatly; I still do.

"My heroes were mostly artists and poets, perhaps because I had grown up with them. The painter, Georgia O'Keeffe, and Stieglitz would drop by when I was a child in France. My heroes were people I had known. I didn't have to go outside for them. Then, too, I guess I always planned to be a heroine myself—in fact I had a firm conviction I would be.

"But I became sidetracked so often, decided to tackle this or that instead of adhering to my original ambition, which was to be a doctor. I seriously considered becoming a concert pianist, but just as with poetry, I knew I would never be a great one and lost interest. It's curious, because the pattern repeated itself over and over again. I was obviously given the potential to do not one thing but many. That is a wonderful but painful burden. When I took an aptitude test I scored tremendously high in a number of things, but there was no one occupation or pursuit which seemed to stand out from the others.

"In my late twenties I took aptitude tests for three days, and it was explained to me that I should choose a profession in which I could incorporate all my interests, or as many as possible. They warned me that if I didn't do this, I would become restless and fail to succeed at anything; I would jump from this to that without fulfilling any one aptitude and simply exhaust all my talents and potential. I realized that this was true, and I feel today that I'm able to combine almost all of my interests in the work I do now—medicine, writing, public speaking. The only talent I don't seem to utilize now is music, and I find I don't miss it at all.

"My first year at Vassar, I settled down happily to pre-medical courses, but by the time my junior year came around I was absolutely fed up with all that chemistry. I had completed all the pre-med, so by my senior year I took only drama and music courses. That's when I began to get interested in acting.

"Then, when I graduated from Vassar, I studied with the American Laboratory Theater for three years. I truly felt I had left medicine behind. I was completely caught up in the theater. I loved it. A number of fabulous people were connected with the Laboratory Theater: Maria Ouspenskaya, Harold Hecht, George Macready, Stella Adler, Boleslavski himself.

"We were very solemn and egotistical about it all. I was dreadfully serious about my new career. I never for a moment felt I would go back to medicine. I always threw myself into my new pursuits wholeheartedly, until the time came when I saw I couldn't be first-rate. And when I say first-rate, I mean first-rate. I identified with Katharine Cornell. She was my idol. If I couldn't be another Katharine Cornell, then I didn't want any part of it. In terms of artistic achievement I could never bear to be second-rate.

"Besides, I had married and had two little girls, one of whom died at the age of eight. It seemed time to put an end to my career on the stage. And I began to notice that theater people were tremendously self-centered. They always talked about theater, couldn't talk about anything else. It was too limited an environment for me. Still, I counted my three years on the stage as very interesting and fruitful ones, years that taught me a lot which is valuable to me today. I learned diction and voice projection, pacing and contrast, all things which help me in public speaking now. Nothing is ever wasted. I needed those three years to test myself—there's that word again—and I was able to plunge in and do it.

"I was much more ready for medicine when I eventually went back to it, at thirty-one, than I would have been earlier. Before, I would have been restless and unprepared. When you are prepared for what you want to do it seems very easy. By the time I got to P&S Medical School at Columbia University, I had a child to raise alone, for I was divorced by then. I finished Medical School at Rochester University and then went to Columbia University School of Public Health. All this didn't seem difficult; my father helped me financially and emotionally. Things got done. If I hadn't allowed myself time to test myself, who knows what might have happened? I was a late starter in every way. Because I had a second family I never even began to practice my profession till I was fifty!

"Most important, I've used my aptitudes for science in the special fields of family planning and sex education in which I've worked. In my eleven years as Medical Director for the Planned Parenthood Federation of America, I was able to establish family planning as a medical service. I worked especially hard on this as a member of the American Medical Association's Committee on Human Reproduction.

"Then, two years ago, I helped found SIECUS because I believe that responsible parenthood, important as it is, is really only a part of a much larger whole, responsible sexuality. I have a passion for scientific truth, and now I'd like to direct it toward clearing away the mythologies and fears that surround human sexual behavior. It's important for us to understand ourselves better as sexual beings. Men and women must learn better ways of relating to each other.

[164]

"In all of this I find myself, in my sixty-third year, primarily motivated by my belief as a Quaker that there is something of God in every person. This is why I value so much being a member of a Family Life Commission of the National Council of Churches of Christ. It is also why I feel one of my greatest opportunities is meeting with young people. Don't believe a word against this generation: it's a splendid one, with real intelligence and integrity. It deserves our trust, and it deserves to share what knowledge we have about human sexuality as a health entity.

"I think the teenagers of this generation are wonderful, I feel I can relate to them. I haven't been to some of the very intellectual schools like Reed, Antioch, Harvard or Radcliffe. For all I know they might tear me apart, but in the university atmosphere I have encountered only bright, committed young people who are eager to come out of the segregated compartments our society has placed them in. They are a great generation. They have escaped the malaise of the college generation which just preceded them, the kids who followed close on the heels of the war and grew up to think that it was square to care about anything. These young people want to know and feel and be of service to the community. They are starting where we left off.

"I haven't been to the ghetto groups, either. I feel it would be presumptuous of me, with my middle-class framework, to go and talk *to* them until I am ready to go and talk *with* them and find out what they want and need, find it out from them. Society outside the ghetto is still wrestling with its own attitudes on sex. We're not yet ready to counsel people whose whole lives have been very deprived and lived in completely different patterns. First, we have to learn how to talk with them without being offensive or condescending, or giving the impression that we are. This is a tremendous group that we haven't even learned how to communicate with on anything.

"SIECUS is such a young organization that we're still having to struggle with the problems of bread and butter. After two years I'm getting my first salary. Hopefully we will get public support in the next few years that will help us to expand our services and program. There's so much to do."

Dr. Calderone asked her secretary to bring me copies of some of her writings, and when I had taken them, she rose to say goodbye. Standing beside her, I was surprised to notice that she was not as tall as I'd thought. With an incandescent smile she said, "I've enjoyed this. Everyone likes to talk about himself to a good listener."

Betsey Johnson

Betsey Johnson came to New York in 1964 as a guest editor for Mademoiselle *magazine. She had a degree from Syracuse University* (magna cum laude *and Phi Beta Kappa*), *a huge portfolio and a lot of self-confidence.*

Eighteen months later she had established herself as one of the bright young designers at a determinedly mod boutique, Paraphernalia, which began as one store in New York and has expanded across the United States. Within six months there was a Johnson explosion: Julie Christie bought countless ver-

sions of the Basic Betsey dress; Anouk Aimée deserted Chanel for Paraphernalia clothes by Betsey Johnson; and pictures of Betsey Johnson outfits were in newspapers and magazines on both sides of the Atlantic. In London, where mod fashion began, the Daily Mail described her as "the best new designer in the United States today."

Betsey Johnson was born in Wethersfield, Connecticut, on August 10, 1942. As a child she studied dancing and by the time she was a sophomore in high school, she was teaching a dance class of her own. She visited New York often and planned to combine art and dance studies there after high school. A year of all-day art classes at the Pratt Institute in Brooklyn and, at night, dance classes in Manhattan helped her resolve the conflict: she transferred to Syracuse University where she finished as an art major. With this background and the guest editorship at Mademoiselle, she slipped into designing.

Ease of movement is perhaps the hallmark of all Betsey Johnson designs. Dresses, pants, tops, bottoms and everything else are cut to do one thing, move with the wearer. She discards whatever she thinks is useless—"darts, folds, pleats and all that junk." She is responsible for the Underwear dress, the See-Through dress, the Do-It-Yourself-with-Big-Plastic-Discs dress, the Bathing Suit dress, the Mirror dress, the Long John Silver (essentially, silver long johns), the Fluorescent dress and, of course, the Basic Betsey. That is a skinny dress of bias-cut jersey with high armholes and an A-line, thigh-high skirt.

These clothes are as bold as their names, but are always easy to wear. Miss Johnson dislikes whatever is "safe" and detests whatever is uncomfortable. A famous picture of a Johnson dress, in Vogue magazine, had the model sitting on a motorcycle. She not only looked comfortable, but she was. "I make clothes that move," says Miss Johnson.

[169]

Betsey Johnson

B ETSEY JOHNSON wheeled a bicycle into her office. She was followed by a blond Afghan puppy that looked plaintive and slightly bewildered. She put the bicycle against a bank of shelves and turned around to look out at the roofs and smoke-stacks and blank walls that are the view from her office win-dow. The office itself is a cubbyhole tucked behind the cutting room of her section of Paraphernalia, a young-clothes outfit with headquarters in the middle of the New York garment district. Taking off her camel coat, she hung it on a pipe rack next to a feather boa, a military band jacket, a tutu and several satin gowns of the Thirties, and began to explain her afternoon.

"The bank took longer than I thought it would and then I had to find food for Kischka. I bought him because he was beautiful. I don't even like dogs, and he was neurotic when he was three months old, but now he's seven months old and it's worse. They're very dependent." She took a white delicatessen package out of her coat pocket and unwrapped it. "There,

Kischka, *eat.*" Kischka whimpered. "He gets liverwurst and roast beef, I get a hard-boiled egg. I'm dieting."

She was wearing a low-necked bulky sweater, blue and red, and camel bell-bottom pants. Her sneakers looked well-worn.

"I like to be interviewed. There was a radio man here a while back, but he was very serious and it was hard to talk to him straight. Could we listen to that interview, since you have the recorder here? No, neither one of us has the time. Where do you want to start?"

"Anywhere."

"I wanted to be a Broadway professional, Ethel Merman-type dancer, so I was always in New York. I came to study. I kind of learned that early about competition, about rat-racing, about the whole New York thing of pushing your way to the front of the line.

"The competition really is the best in New York for dancing, for design, for everything—more so than in Paris, London, anywhere. I've always believed that, for me anyway (I have this ego kind of thing), I would rather give the hardest game a try and maybe not win, not make out okay, and in the end say, 'Well, I can't make it in New York, it's too much for me, I'm not that good, I'm not that talented, I'm not physically and mentally able to make it in New York. And so if I can't I'll be very happy to go somewhere else.' But it was always very important to me to *try* to make it here, because I think New York is the only place, especially for design, for the really commercial fields. Dedication is important, of course, in dancing, theater, design, fashion. You have to be at the commercial center.

"But at sixteen I had to achieve some kind of personal glory, and dancing—I love the feeling of being on a stage more than anything in the world. There was such a great feeling in being there with the orchestra and the lights, such a feeling of glory and happiness. Whatever I did, I had to come out on top. It's like that great feeling on the stage.

"At the same time, I was interested in art. I made jewelry, things like that. In dancing school I averaged seven to ten costumes a year. Mother would make the costumes for me, and I would copy them for my dolls. I've always been interested in how things went together, in making things, which is why I love designing. You can be the director, and really flashy New York-type dressing is very theatrical, made for entrances, parties, excitement."

I had an image of the pages of *Vogue,* the covers of *Bazaar*—vinyl, bare, wild clothes. But Miss Johnson was talking about dancing again.

"I ran a dancing school my sophomore year in high school. I had to design and make costumes for all the recitals. Fourteen kids in the class meant fourteen costumes. That meant I had to order the yardage from a fabric house in New York, find the patterns, everything. You know, I was organized that way."

Whatever kind of organization Miss Johnson was talking about, it was her own special kind. Her office looked as if it would burst at the seams if she tried to find a place for anything more. Broad horizontal shelves in the corner held portfolios, magazines and what looked like a series of old lunches—delicatessen wrappers, a crust of bread, coffee containers. Old costume jewelry littered every surface, spilling over a desk whose main feature was a round fat paper tub of Crayolas. All over the wall she had tacked up Crayola drawings of her designs and labeled them: "Bare Things," "Tops and Bottoms," "Little Things." On the wall were photographs of herself, of models in Betsey Johnson dresses, of assorted children. Everything in the room was Betsey.

"There's my kind of organization and a businessman's—those

black lines on the white paper, all those file cabinets. I have my own system. For the dancing school I had my own studio, my own piano player. I had people collecting money, making costumes. I organized recitals, so there it was. I taught Monday evenings and all my Saturdays, but I always had art going in high school, too. I was always *the* best artist.

"And I knew I had to organize myself to get into college, to keep up my grades and direct myself there. There had to be college, because I wasn't old enough to go from high school to New York, and I didn't have enough confidence in dancing to take me straight to dancing school. And I really wanted college. I'd been a cheerleader, been active in student government, clubs, plays, all that. And I wanted, if I was going to college, to get a great, great education. The thing is, if you graduate from a second-rate school, you won't get that great a job, but if you graduate from a top art school like Pratt, where I started out, you have a great job practically assured.

"I went to art school to study dancing. There's no place for dancing except a city like New York, so I went to Pratt and took dance lessons at lunch hours and in the evenings. But in a professional art school like Pratt, you've got classes all day long, and I'd get out of my dancing lesson at two in the morning. Still, I kept a high average. I was a cheerleader, too, and at a big art school that is really something. I was sort of the rah-rah artist, and they hated that, because at Pratt they thought that to be a good artist you had to think of nothing else. They couldn't knock me in the art school, though, because I had my good marks and I really worked hard, but I needed this other stuff too. They couldn't see why I would want to be involved with cheerleading. But what they didn't realize about me—and I think it's true about a lot of kids—is that I have to play hard so that I work harder, and cheerleading took up some of this extra energy that I just had to use.

"I finally decided that I should transfer to a large university. I didn't feel I was meeting enough people at Pratt, that I was being exposed to enough. I saw the same thirty kids day in and day out, the same little surroundings, one city block, the same everything. And I could be serious about my art without being around the art school atmosphere continually, you know. I don't need that much of a push from my surroundings. So I transferred to Syracuse, a big college with a big art school where they don't push so much.

"I don't know where the urge to compete comes from. Maybe from the family. I'm the middle one. I was more catered to than my brother, who was two years younger, or my sister, who was two years older. I was always in the lime-light, getting attention. My sister's very different, very quiet. If Sally wanted attention, she'd have had to overpower me or outshine me or something, because I was so theatrical. She didn't care about that. She's straight and open-minded and creative—she has it in her head, while I can get it outside and translate it into clothes or something. It's rougher for her to translate; she doesn't want to give up the living-in-the-country-happy-with-the-children kind of life. Her energy is for her home and her child; I have it for my work. I competed with my brother and sister. There's just a lot of energy in us, you know. The Johnson family always managed to be outstanding.

"My parents think of themselves as successful, too, and I think they are. My father graduated from Pratt—he's an engineer—and my mother works in the high school in Wethersfield, Connecticut. She's in guidance there, and helps the kids. My parents are very proud of us. We always come out on top somehow. My sister and I competed for everything. She was the social chairman of the junior prom, the princess of the

Spring Festival, and I had to do all that too. I really felt I had to keep up with her.

"I wasn't very close to my brother or my sister until I got away from them, until we separated as a family. Now my sister is married and has a child and is teaching and she's very open-minded, and says, 'That crazy Betsey, she does things like that, let her do them,' but my parents haven't let go yet. I am at the point where they are great people and friends and like that, but they have this kind of parental hang-up. I'm still their daughter and might still be able to be influenced about what kind of men I should meet, what kind of an apartment I should live in. My parents are very happy with what I'm doing, with my success, but they don't like New York. They don't understand New York, financially, socially. They just don't understand it, period.

"My parents aren't exactly the impressible kind. I never got praise from them, especially not my mother. She isn't at all like a theatrical mother. None of this 'Come on, Betsey, get to dancing class,' or 'You were wonderful, darling.' She never bragged about me. I never heard her praise me, I never hear her praise me now. I find out through my relatives that my parents are very proud. My aunts and my other relatives know what I'm doing, right up to date."

She was pacing the room by now—there wasn't a lot of room to pace—and looking worried. Her hands are like a little girl's, a tomboy's, close-bitten fingernails and a little grubby. She put them on her hips and spoke as from a small pedestal.

"I didn't start out to be a fashion designer at all, but I wanted to do some kind of art work. I was always very flexible. First I wanted to be a children's book illustrator. I took everything I could think of at Syracuse—fabric design, fashion illustration, figure drawing—and everything helped in the long

[176]

run. Any experience, good or bad, helps you in your work. After you learn to paint a bowl that looks like a bowl, you have to learn to see into situations and people, too. You can't draw out on paper any more than you have in your own life.

"With me, nothing I was doing in college began to pull together until I entered this contest. I love contests, always have, any little kind of game, and somehow I always win. In my senior year my roommate persuaded me to enter the *Mademoiselle* magazine Guest Editor contest. It was the first one I really cared about winning, because it would bring me to New York. I didn't think about making it straight to the top after college. Just being a runaround girl in a fashion magazine, anything as long as I was on the scene—that was enough for a beginning. If I could win this contest, I could get to New York and be an assistant to one of the editors for a month. Maybe there'd be an opening, maybe something would break. At least I'd be taken care of for a month. They set you up in a hotel, they introduce you to all kinds of people. I'd be started out.

"I really hated to enter it, because I never dreamed I'd win it, and it was the first one I cared about winning. And it was one of those things that go on for months and months: 'Keep going, we like your work, here's the latest issue of *Mademoiselle,* send us an essay on what you thought of it.' They bugged you so much you couldn't forget it. I wanted to forget all about it, but I sent them all their little things, and then I heard I was in the semi-finals, then the finals. And all of a sudden one day I got a telegram that I'd won. I had to miss my graduation exercises. They flew me to New York, and they made me assistant fabric editor!

"I was *furious.* I guess it's very hard for *Mademoiselle* to find someone to be fabric editor, and because I'd taken fabric design in college and did these big splashy prints and made clothes out of them, they thought, 'Aha! We have someone for the fabric department.' So they threw me in there, and I was so mad because it had nothing to do with art. I wanted to get close to the art department. Boy, did I work—in at nine o'clock, doing the editor's fabric files. I got to know every fabric house, every fabric, different weaves, different blends. There was so much work that I was kept on for another month.

"And while I was making a little salary at *Mademoiselle*, I took my portfolio around to places during my lunch hour. The very first man I saw was this guy at McGraw-Hill. He looked at my book, and he said, 'What do you want to do?' And I said, 'Me? What do you mean? *I* don't know what I want to do.' There I was with that portfolio—every different kind of work in it, the fabric designs, the fashion illustrations, and everything looked like it had been done by a different artist. I'd done everything to please all my instructors, to get my little A. He said I'd really have to work hard to get my own style, because that's the only thing for a person to have in a professional field; it has to be very personal, unique.

"He said I could be very successful in this city, and quickly, too. *I*'d always believed that if you're going to be good, it doesn't take ten, twenty years to get there. If you've got it you can do it in five years at the most. New York is too hard on you physically and mentally to knock yourself out for ten years. So he said I could do it in like two years, but in those two years I'd have to work so hard. He really got very emotional: 'Tears, sweat, blood!' I didn't know what he meant by that kind of work. But now, well, it's all very lovely now. I sit here and have tea and talk, but my first year after the two months at *Mademoiselle* I got a job as runaround girl in an art department. That didn't pay me enough money, so I had a sweater business. I made sweaters and got mail orders. I made three hundred of those things by hand. But I wanted more work, so I started up a fashion illustration business, and there was a lot of response. I worked nine to five, I had to make a sweater every night—that took four hours—and a minimum of four on the weekends, I had to do the fashion illustration assignments, keep up my own portfolio, and I was making my own clothes.

"When I think of how hard I worked—I could count the parties I went to and the people I knew on one hand. But I was so happy. In New York everything is exaggerated. If you do something here, you get such a great feeling if it's the least bit successful. Whereas if I were in, say, Wethersfield, Connecticut, and I did something, who'd know about it? There's just not the same satisfaction. I do have something to offer people and I want to offer it to as many people as I can. For that I must be in New York."

She fiddled with her tea bag. Her legs were hiked over the arms of her chair.

"The thing about New York is that there are so many opportunities here, something has to work for you if you try hard enough. If you have something to offer people, they don't care how old you are. A forty-year-old designer can sit down and design what she thinks a sixteen-year-old wants to wear to a prom, but all of a sudden the big businessman, the big design houses, have realized that no one knows better than a sixteen-year-old who goes to a prom what that sixteen-year-old wants to wear. The trick is not just to have some vague idea, but to have the skills, the craft, the ability to produce for these people. I just happened to have it.

"It wasn't always possible for kids to sell themselves, though. I remember when I was doing the sweaters, I went around to design houses and no one would dream of hiring someone my age. But Paul Young, the president of Paraphernalia, believes we know what's happening, believes in giving us a chance. There's something about when you're young, and he knows it.

"People may think I'm being catty, but you have to keep telling employers what you can offer them. You don't treat people commercially—that's not the way to do it. I wanted to do fashion illustrations for *Mademoiselle*, but I couldn't go up to the art director and say 'I want to work for you. Look at my book.' What happened was that I was asked to dinner at the house of the editor of *Mademoiselle*. She adores old-fashioned drawings of shoes, so for a thank-you note I sent her one of my drawings, this wild shoe, and she flipped over it. She ran into the art director the next day, and said, 'Why don't you let Betsey do some shoe illustrations? Let her try.' It's always better to let other people think they're discovering you. You don't prove to people that you can do fashion illustration, but that you want to do something for *them*.

"When you're young and just starting out, you can't expect money, royal treatment. You should just be happy you're being given a chance. Money is what you get after a while, after you see the company is making a profit from you, then maybe you get a business manager. I should be a businessman, but I'm not. I remember not caring about money in the beginning, I was so happy to be doing what I wanted to do. A lot of kids want big money right away, because their parents have taught them that money is security. My parents are still saying that, parents never stop it. Like in high school: 'Dropouts never get a job that pays enough money,' 'Save your money,' 'Remember the rainy days.'

"Right now I'm used to the money, of course, because I know I couldn't live as I want to or have the things I like without it. There's a freedom to having money. But when I think of what really makes me happy, it has nothing to do with money. And for the first time in a long while I'm not scared about where it's coming from. I know I can't cut myself off from my parents entirely, the way some kids can. I don't have enough in the bank. But I know I can earn money. Even if I lose this job, I know I can do something to keep me in food and rent and the things I want.

"Of course now that my designs really make a profit for Paraphernalia, I find myself getting catty, thinking about the percentage I should be getting for the work I do. What are the other designers making? That sort of thing is very bad. When all you're doing is just using your chance, money isn't on your mind. You're working for the work.

"It's different now. I need a business manager. But it's such a family here, I hate to get businesslike with people who are, like, my friends. It's very hard to say okay, now we're friends, and boom, now it's business, like Jekyll and Hyde. That's hard to do.

"I couldn't have thought of myself as a big New York success at sixteen; I was too caught up in what I was doing right then. Kids want to be liked; when you're young you don't know yourself well enough to be sure what they'll want in five years, or two years, or even six months. Kids need security. That's why they all dress alike.

"I was a very normal—normal, what's normal?—kid, but I really liked planning and making things work. I wasn't a child prodigy, I didn't go home and sketch madly and paint fantastic things in the cellar. I was just a successful little high-school kid. I wanted people to like me, and I liked having lots of girlfriends and boyfriends. I was the exaggerator, things were always extra extra extra great or extra extra horrible.

"And that's still true now. What's good to me is really good, and what's bad, what's not me, forget it. The only reason I'm any good and where I am now is that I did what I wanted to do. I know it's more important for me to design what I feel I should design, even if I do the worst things in the world and get fired for it. And when I do bad things I expect to get fired, especially if they don't sell. But if I get fired, it will be because I did what I wanted to do and it just wasn't right, it was bad.

"It's like going over a bridge. One side is doing things because it makes *them* happy, pleases *them*. The other side is your own need to do what makes *you* happy. It takes a long time to get from one side of the bridge to the other. If you want to keep your job, you have to keep people happy. But you get to the point where making yourself happy is most important because you have to be important to yourself. I don't want to say something in design that someone else can say. If I did that, there'd be no point in my being around. That's why I won't ever get into a mass-production kind of junior sportswear house and do pants suits just like everyone else's, because they'd have no real need for *me*. I might as well drop out.

"Even in high school I couldn't stand art teachers who took your pencil to show you how to draw, who'd draw an apple on the board and want you to copy it. I was very selfish. I hated that kind of thing. With what I do now, too, I want it to my design, my fabric. If it's wrong, I have to take the whole blame. I can't put it off on someone else. So many times there are pressures from the outside. Like here at Paraphernalia, they want you to design this kind of dress, they want you to use this fabric. You can just go so far in conforming to their ideas. But in the end, if you design a dress for a magazine and it's horrible, you can say, 'Why did I ever listen to them?' but on the other hand you can blame them, 'I never liked that fabric anyway.' You can kind of pass the buck. But if what you've done is successful and you can't take every ounce of success personally, you're not happy about it. If you've done the design and someone else picked out the fabric, it's not the same thing. I have a real greedy kind of ego—there are lots of different kinds of egos and mine is the selfish, greedy kind. I never want to go halfway with anything. I want to be very rich or very poor, to live in the middle of the city or in the high mountains, to use chrome, paper, plastic for dresses if I want to. All the way.

"That's why I never lasted with boyfriends. I'd get very tired of them. A boy has to be able to keep up with me. Sometimes, my head goes so fast that I talk in half sentences, but I just expect that the person knows what I'm after. At sixteen I had crushes and boyfriends, and I went steady for a year or so. My boyfriends really had to be great-looking—a star basketball player, a great guy. In a way I was competing with my boyfriends. If they couldn't make it with me, well—so long.

"My parents would like me to find a very organized, steady, business type. They've never liked my boyfriends, except for my high-school steady. They liked him. But there are too many of me for that kind of unimaginative type to keep up with—me nine to five, what's driving me in fashion design. But then there's the me that's sensitive and perceptive, so that the men I get along with best now are those who are trying to express themselves too—photographers, artists, musicians. We understand our drives for our work, but we understand, too, that we're very sensitive, even though we have to make out in the commercial kind of New York atmosphere. We can't just hang around and go to clubs at night and go discothequing. We have to get from each other what we can't get in the daytime at work, and there's not much time.

"In my work, from the dancing school on, I've always had to deal with older people. I was the same age as a lot of my pupils. I worked with their parents as equals. Now everyone I work with is almost twice my age, so I'd rather stay home and read and be by myself than be with crowds of people. In high school I needed to be one of the group, but now I've become very selective. I'd rather be with one person, myself, than be with crowds of people. It's part of a kind of self-confidence I've developed. It's only in the last three months that I've been able to say, 'Well, if *Vogue* doesn't like my sketches I don't care a hang.' You should have interviewed me last year, it would have been really interesting. I have confidence now in my work, and in myself, that I've just acquired in the last couple of months.

"I'm twenty-four and I'm not afraid of being fired tomorrow. I can always do something else. You know, I've realized that it's just making yourself happy. I could be very happy now in a home, with a husband and a child. I'd always be making doorknobs or something—I'd be a crazy kind of housewife, creating so much junk. I do want to get married some day. It's hard for me, but I have to figure out time for another person. All along there was only me, you know, and now it can't be time for my family. It has to be time for someone who's very close to me, and that's a big problem to work out, because I've never thought about what someone else does during the day, and how *he* feels and what *he* wants to talk about tonight.

"I went through being pinned and going steady and all, and I didn't get married in that big panic thing after you graduate from high school because I was just too selfish. You have to get through that break after high school into college, and after college until you're on your own. Those are the two places when most people end up married, whether they're ready or not. But I was too interested in myself. I was until I met the boy I'm going with now. On one hand, I would just like to go home at night, work on my apartment and fool around. On the other hand, I want to be with him. That's what's really rough, trying to balance out my own personal life with someone else's life. And that's important to me now, because I don't want to be fifty years old and a haggard, worn-out old designer. Just designing is not the answer. It's time for me to work just as hard on my own personality as at designing. I really am trying to be happy in all phases of my life.

"And I still am very caught up in my work. But it's really miserable sometimes. You're exploited, and it happens all the time. Last year, for instance, I was sending out fashion illustrations to magazines, dresses shown with shoes, hats, stockings. And people said, 'Betsey, don't do it, they'll pick those sketches right up and knock off those shoes.' They were right, too. And for a while I stopped putting feet in the sketches. But it's good exercise for me to think of the whole look, everything about a garment and what it can do. So I just said, 'Nuts,' and started putting the feet back in. I have to keep exercising myself to stay on top of my own ideas, so I can't be bothered about every imitator that comes along. I think of a T-shirt dress, and if there's another T-shirt dress in *Mademoiselle* or *Glamour* next month, well, tough luck. And the same goes for the total look. If zigzag ribbed stockings look great with my designs, and someone picks them up and knocks them off, I just have to shrug. I worry about running out of ideas, but that's a waste of energy. I can just hope that the ideas I do have keep being right. So far I've been lucky, and I still believe that I have a feel for what people, especially young people like me, really want: things that move, that can be moved in, things that are bright and easy and that give a feeling for the total person in them, things that are a little dangerous.

"Most fashion books, fashion notes, even fashion magazines for young people are always talking about what's safe, what to do that won't embarrass you or bother other people. Fashion models have always known, though, that to succeed they must find out what's best for them. So they have to spend a lot of time looking at themselves. That's what everybody should do who's interested in looking great, instead of trying to find some kind of formula. I'm in design because I don't believe there's a formula for good looks or chic, and I think more and more people are beginning to know that the best way to look good is to look like yourself."

She grinned—without doubt, the real Betsey Johnson—and said, "I think we're ready to look like who we really are or want to be, to break loose a little."

Mary Dublin Keyserling

There was special justice in President Johnson's appointment of Mrs. Mary Dublin Keyserling as Director of the Women's Bureau of the Department of Labor in 1964. Ever since her graduation from Barnard College, Mrs. Keyserling has been a splendid example of how a professional woman can contribute skills, intelligence and energy to the nation.

Mary Dublin was born in 1910 in New York City. Her father was the Statistician and subsequently Vice-President of the Metropolitan Life Insurance Company. Miss Dublin's own first job after college was as a staff member on the Committee on Costs of Medical Care. Then, after working for the New York State Charities Aid Association, she went to Europe, where she did graduate work at the London School of Economics. When she returned to the United States, she studied further at Columbia University, earning her Ph.D. degree, and then joined the faculty of Sarah Lawrence College. There, from 1933 to 1938, she taught economics and statistics.

Like many young teachers of the 1930's, Miss Dublin saw excitement and opportunity in public affairs. In 1938, she left the academic life to become executive secretary of the National Consumers' League. She married Leon Keyserling, then General Counsel of the United States Housing Authority, in 1940, and they made their home in Washington, D.C.

The skills Mrs. Keyserling had devoted to public welfare and the consumer in peacetime were soon to serve wartime America. Her first Washington job was to coordinate hearings for a special House Committee on National Defense Migration. After the United States entered World War II, she served as a top economist in the Office of Civil Defense and in the Foreign Economics Administration.

During the Truman Administration, while Mr. Keyserling became chairman of the Council of Economic Advisers, Mrs. Keyserling continued in government service in the Commerce Department's Office of International Trade. She resigned from this post in 1953.

Before her appointment as Director of the Women's Bureau in 1964, she worked as a consulting economist and lecturer; she was elected President of the Women's National Democratic Club for 1963–64.

The Keyserlings now live on a tree-lined street in the northwest section of Washington.

Mary Dublin Keyserling

This is very exciting, to be asked to discuss how times have changed since I was sixteen. I would suspect that life has changed more for women in the period of years since I was sixteen than at any other comparable period in history. That's a very strong statement, but if you think about it, you'll realize it's true."

The woman speaking so assuredly was Mrs. Mary Dublin Keyserling, Director of the Women's Bureau of the United States Department of Labor, in Washington, D.C. Near at hand were stacks upon stacks of documents and papers which could undoubtedly have proved what she had just said. But, looking at me with vivacious blue eyes, she seemed pleased to talk more personally about changing times and her sixteenth year. She chose her words with care, often fingering meditatively the bright Mexican necklace that encircled her throat.

"At sixteen," she said, "I was already in college, at Barnard. I feel my ambitions were very much like any other girl's in many ways. I looked ahead to marriage, of course, because I think all young women feel this is the most important ambition in their lives. And I agree. I took it for granted that I'd marry and I anticipated having a family, but—and this is a very real but—I always assumed I would combine marriage and a career, which was rather unusual in those days. Most girls thought they might work for a while after finishing school, but once they were married they felt that their families would be a full-time job. Only adversity would bring them back to the labor force.

"Still, there was a growing group of girls who felt that it might be possible to make a success of marriage and a career, both. It was a small group, but it existed. Shall I admit how long ago this was? It was forty years ago, when I was sixteen, and what a change we've seen.

"Now, nearly half of all our adult women hold jobs. It's a gigantic difference. Forty-seven percent of all our women between the ages of eighteen and sixty-four are working. A great many of them are working by choice. This is partly because the change in standards of living have made it possible for girls to stay in school, continue their training and look ahead to careers. Since 1940, the standard of living of the average American family has more than doubled, and girls needn't go out to work at a very young age to contribute to the family's income so much any more. Eighty percent of our youngsters graduate from high school today; three times as many girls graduate today as did when I was sixteen, and more than three times as many graduate from college. So girls today have never-before-realized opportunities—to find their abilities, cultivate them, know more about the world around them. All this means they can contribute more to society. The number of women on the job today in volunteer and community work, with civic responsibilities—it's really one of the most dramatic social changes to occur in this country in decades.

"Forty years ago, even at Barnard, which tends to be an intellectually oriented school, a girl who actively planned on a career was very much the exception. I myself didn't know precisely what it was I wanted to do, but I did have an immense interest in the life around me and in the idea of improving the standard of living for everybody. I believed it was very important for me to help make this a better world.

"I have to admit, though, that, interested as I was in economics and social science, I was terribly intrigued with the theater. I enjoyed acting in plays at school, or writing or directing them. I seriously considered becoming an actress or a playwright, and up until the time I was eighteen or nineteen I honestly couldn't have said what I'd do. I thought of it as a tremendous decision I'd have to make, but in looking back I realize that the decision was pretty well made without my knowing it. I just *was* committed to social science, even when I was most active in theater. But my interest in the theater didn't disappear; it became, rather, an embellishment of life while the other became my life's work.

"Oh, but I remember the excitement of being sixteen and in a city like New York with all its wonderful museums and theaters. I remember hoarding my pennies and sitting up in the gallery at every play I could possibly get to, and I remember going to museums and art galleries every Saturday morning and feeling so breathless and excited by what I saw. I discovered the world of classical music then, and so many other things, the things you absorb and delight in when you are sixteen and find the world opening up for you. I can't think of anything more wonderful—the sense of discovery!

"When I was seventeen I was very privileged to be taken to Europe by my parents. They were extremely busy, and I often had to amuse myself. I used to go to the galleries in Paris, and I remember the feeling I had when I first saw the Impressionists. You suddenly know that there's so much that's wonderful and rich to learn about. You realize there's just not time enough to do everything, to study and to learn all you want to learn about music and art, to explore all the avenues of life. It's a very wonderful and poignant moment when you realize this.

"I was a great romantic, too, when I was sixteen. My heroes and heroines at the time were a mixture of romantic fantasy and passionate admiration for the people who were effecting social reform. Politically, my greatest hero was Alfred E. Smith, and I greatly admired Jane Addams and Lillian Wald for what they were trying to do. At the same time, I loved Shelley and Keats, Byron and Swinburne. They were real stars in my firmament.

"But what better time for romanticism than when you are sixteen? To be aware of the pattern the world is taking and to set out to prepare a role for yourself doesn't mean you can't have the natural romanticism every teenager feels. Life is so diversified, there's room for every joy. I cannot comprehend how anybody can live a life in which there's one moment of boredom.

"When I was sixteen I had every confidence. I truly felt I'd be able to make a good life for myself. I owe much of this to my parents, who instilled in us the feeling that we must use our lives wisely and be of service. It was always taken for granted. And I had the great advantage of having parents who felt that women should have exactly the same opportunities and advantages as men. This went so far in our family that there were no jobs designated for the two boys or for the two girls. Whatever had to be done in the household just had to be done. There was no idea that certain work was women's work or men's work; it was shared. If there were dishes to be done, they were done by the child whose turn it was. The same was true of gardening or anything else.

"There was no concept of separate roles for us, you see. I was a very feminine child, yet one summer when I was about twelve, I was the boss of the family carpentry shop. My brothers were no less masculine for having washed dishes when they were boys. We were all so fortunate in having this extraordinary upbringing when we were young. And today adults are taking the sex labels off jobs too, more and more. In our homes husbands and wives are participating more equally in rearing the children and sharing the household jobs. Most of the young men I know are just as good with their children as the mothers are. This is becoming the pattern in American life, and the early training my sister and brothers and I had was, in fact, a preparation for life.

"That's why I hope young girls today will try and get the absolute maximum of education. With possibilities for girls so wide open, to drop out of school is to condemn oneself to a life which is unnecessarily handicapped and dull. Oh, it's true there are other ways to get training and experience. Many teenagers are so anxious for practical experience that they drop out of school, but practical experience comes soon enough. Life is long, and it's lengthening for all of us.

"When I was born, the average girl baby could expect to live a little more than fifty years. Now the life expectancy is approximately seventy-five. This is a gift of twenty-five years, on the average, for my generation, and being seventy-five or eighty today is very different than it was in my grandmother's time. Women that age today are healthier and far more active. And because life is long, we shouldn't be in too much of a hurry for practical experience. In the privileged atmosphere of a school, a girl can learn things which affect her whole life. It's a chance to read and explore the beauties of literature, the practicalities as well as the beauties of thought. And, of course, in the world we are building now there will be little room for people without the sort of skills that come with a good education. I am speaking of skills which lead to success in life. I don't mean financial success, but success as the Greeks defined it: 'Happiness is the exercise of vital powers along lines of excellence in a life affording them scope.' In other words, we are happy when we have found and developed our own abilities to the point of excellence and used them fully.

"And of course we must now consider not only the use of our vital powers but the use of them to make life more worthwhile for others as well as ourselves. Our world provides so many opportunities for giving, for helping others. Parents can instill this idea in very young children just by making them aware of it.

"I think my parents managed to do this with their children. There were four of us—I had one sister and two brothers—and my parents felt that children should grow up in the country; they considered the city too confining and wanted us to have room to play and ramble. So when we were all quite small the family moved to the most distant part of Westchester County, which was still quite farmlike and open. It was a wonderful life. But when we grew a little older and they began to think of educational opportunities for us, they felt that we should have the better schooling a city can provide. We moved back to the city, and I was miserable when we first returned to New York.

"I adored the country and the woods, and I was appalled by the ugliness of city life. There was poverty close at hand, and I yearned for the openness and beauty of the country. My mother sensed my unhappiness, and one day, when I was fourteen, she said to me: 'Mary, if you were told that you'd have to spend the rest of your life in a room that was cluttered and messy and untidy, and there was no other alternative but to spend your whole life there, what would you do?' I thought for just a moment and answered, 'Of course, I'd put it in order. I'd be miserable in a messy room, and I'd pick it up and make it as attractive as I could if this is where I was going to be.' My mother looked at me and said: 'You live in this world. If you'll help to make it a more attractive place, I think you'll be a happier person.' I've never quite forgotten that.

"We *can* make the world a place of greater beauty, each in our own way. I think happiness comes in direct proportion to how much we relate to others and give of ourselves. Some do it through wonderful human relations, and I wouldn't minimize this. I am a woman who has elected to have a career, to combine family life with work, partly because I have a great deal of energy, strong intellectual interests and concern for others. The reason I spend my days here as the head of the Women's Bureau is to help enlarge the freedom of choice that's open to all women. Our job is to encourage greater training, employment and service opportunities for women, and to help them make the most of their abilities. I'm not saying that all women should work, but for those who choose to, our job is to help make it possible for them to give of their best and to have the kinds of jobs they will enjoy doing. For those who elect to be homemakers, that is their choice. My sister chose not to work for most of her married life, and she has found fulfillment in rearing her family, and in horticulture. She has become one of this country's leading experts on horticulture, and her garden is one of the most beautiful I've ever seen. My point is, no one would argue that either homemaking or a career is superior, but just that there should always be freedom of choice to do one or the other or combine them both.

"Our sixteen-year-olds should be made aware of all the realities of a woman's life today. Now, girls marry earlier than their mothers and grandmothers did—half of them marry before they are twenty. When I was sixteen, a girl was not allowed to stay in college if she married. I remember a girl who married in her senior year, and we had to keep it just an incredible secret so that she could graduate. How ridiculous. You can see how times have changed. The more educated a girl was then, the less likely she was to marry young.

"Now half of us have had our last child by the time we're thirty. Young women ought to think about this. It means that, on the average, by the time a woman is thirty-five, her last child is in school. By the time she's forty, or even earlier, she has very little left to do at home, yet she is still young and active. She wants her children to have the best education possible, and in many cases the income of the husband isn't enough to put two or three children through college. She wants the family to enjoy the better things in life. So if she has the time and the education, she sees the opportunities around her and the need for her contribution. She has abilities she can use. We will see, more and more, a pattern of women working before marriage, dropping out during the early years of child-raising and then returning to work at forty or even before. The women who went to school in my generation are returning in great numbers to the working world after the age of thirty-five.

"As for me, ever since I first came out of college I have had a succession of absolutely fascinating jobs. My first job was as a research assistant on a comprehensive study of health services —who could afford them, what the deficiencies of hospitals and medical services were. Next I was offered a job with the State Charities Aid Association in New York City, and I followed and reported on legislation in the Senate and Assembly of New York State. Then I was given a fellowship to go on to do graduate studies. I did my graduate work in economics and sociology and statistics at the London School of Economics and at Columbia. After that I taught economics at Sarah Lawrence College for five years, but somehow I felt I didn't want to just talk about social and economic issues. I wanted to be a part of things in a more active way.

"I left teaching in 1938 and have had one very interesting job after another ever since—as Director of the National Consumers League, and later in other private industry and government posts. One year during World War II, I had the rare good fortune to work as an assistant to Mrs. Eleanor Roosevelt.

"If I could say one single thing to the sixteen-year-olds of today it would be: Hitch your wagon to a star. How wonderful to be young and starting, to be in a period when your eyes are opening to all of life. We've made it possible now for more and more young people with ability to go to college, to go as far as they want in school. What I hope more than anything is that everyone who can will take advantage of it. Oh, I think the future will be increasingly rewarding for women."

As Mrs. Keyserling said this, it was five o'clock, and groups of government employees were pouring from the Department of Labor building toward the bus stops on Pennsylvania Avenue. But Mrs. Keyserling's working day had not ended when I rose to leave.

"The only problem," she said, "is that there is so little time. There is never time to do all you would like to do, to keep up your garden or take walks in the woods or read all the books you want to read. We have been granted more time than our grandmothers were able to count on, but the moments go so fast."

Frances Scott Fitzgerald Lanahan

Frances Scott Fitzgerald Lanahan is the only child of F. Scott and Zelda Fitzgerald. Born October 26, 1921, shortly after her father had published his first book, This Side of Paradise, *she spent her early childhood shuttling between the United States and Europe. In 1930, when she was eight, her mother was hospitalized for treatment of the mental illness that was to keep her in and out of hospitals for most of the rest of her life.*

In the years that followed, F. Scott Fitzgerald tried to be both mother and father to his daughter in spite of the serious personal problems that were adversely affecting his literary work. Sometimes he was not an easy parent to live with. But his strictness and good, if omnipresent, advice were motivated by a real concern for her well-being, quite evident in his Letters to His Daughter, *published by Scribner's in 1965. As Zelda Fitzgerald said, he was "always planning happiness for Scottie and me." During her adolescence, Scottie lived part of the time with friends of her father, particularly the Harold Obers. (Mr. Ober was Scott Fitzgerald's literary agent.)*

She was encouraged by her father to excel in academic work, but like her father often found life more compelling than her studies. She entered Vassar College at sixteen and promptly founded a musical comedy organization which took up most of her time. In 1939, at eighteen, she sold her first article to Mademoiselle. *She was graduated from Vassar in 1942, one year after her father's death, and went to work for* Time *magazine.*

In 1943 she married Samuel J. Lanahan, an attorney. They have four children and live in Washington, D.C. Her short stories and articles have been published in House and Garden, Esquire *and* The New Yorker, *among others; and she now writes a weekly column, "News to Me," for* The Washington Post.

Frances Scott Fitzgerald Lanahan

FRANCES FITZGERALD LANAHAN, called "Scottie" by everyone who knows her, came whirling through the door of the Rive Gauche restaurant in Georgetown, a flash of blond hair, emerald dress and imitation leopard coat. She slid in beside me with a breathless hello. "Am I late or are you early?" she asked, with just a faint trace of the South in her voice.

I was early—the shuttle plane from New York to Washington had made good time—but the restaurant was a pleasant place to wait in. The plates in front of me were heavy silver, a vase of bud roses graced every table, and across the aisle sat a four-star general.

Mrs. Lanahan shrugged out of her coat and grinned. "You have to have clams casino to begin with," she said, "they're so good they don't even taste like clams." Through lunch we talked about, among other things, the current new younger generation. I suggested that a new generation comes into being every three or four years. She disagreed—every twenty years was a more accurate measure. "Of course," she said, "the war was the great dividing line. No one has been the same since. Everything that happened before World War II belongs in one category, and everything since in another. My generation—those now in their forties—was the connecting link. We've been growing up while all the tremendous changes were happening.

"When I was sixteen, children lived in a snug world. We had a confidence then which came of total security, providing, of course, you didn't come from a slum area. If you were brought up in the solid American middle or upper class, you had a feeling that nothing could go too far wrong. Everything would turn out right in the end. I'm not sure that exists any more."

Our lunch finished, we came blinking into the bright daylight to drive through the heart of Georgetown to an airy white house built on the edge of a ravine. On entering, Mrs. Lanahan walked through several rooms, opening curtains to let light in. Down in the basement-playroom, she showed me a mural. An entire wall had been painted as a fantasyland of small creatures. Bats in tuxedoes hung upside down from tree branches; squirrels tilting martini glasses peeked out from under fallen logs. "My daughter painted this when *she* was sixteen," said Mrs. Lanahan with visible pride. "It's a forest coming-out party. She'd decided she didn't want to be a debutante, and this was her protest. Now she's an art major at Sarah Lawrence College."

Her daughter's room upstairs had more paintings and sketches. "We've learned to encourage our children, my generation has. Psychiatry has taught us that individuals vary greatly and it's useless to try to force them into set patterns. We lack the rigidity our parents had. Our mistakes are more often in the other direction. Because of Dr. Spock, we are overly shy about even disciplining our children."

"Your house is like a tree house," I said as we went downstairs, passing windows on every side that gave a view of leaves and lawns.

She seemed pleased. "We built it that way. I feel closed in without sun and air; that's why I hate those new hotels with hermetically sealed windows for air conditioning. Let's sit in here." She led me to a long, summery room with many windows. It seemed to be built out over the ravine.

"There are three vast areas which have changed radically in concept from when I was sixteen. First, the idea that you were a scarlet woman if you went to bed with a man before you married him. That was still the assumption when I graduated from Vassar at twenty. Not everyone obeyed it, but it was still the rule.

"Secondly, the concept of God, even for people who weren't religious, was very important. If you weren't religious, you felt uncomfortable. Religion was something you adhered to, a pattern you followed. I hardly know a teenager today who goes to church regularly. Statistically, many do, but compared to the world I grew up in, there have been drastic alterations.

"The third obvious change has to do with the role of women. When I was sixteen, you couldn't really imagine being a successful female unless you were primarily oriented toward wifehood and motherhood. Before World War II a few women went to graduate school and became teachers and lawyers and doctors, but they were the exception. More and more now, we are coming to understand that having children is only part of life. At most it might take twenty years to raise children, and with a life expectancy of at least sixty, that's what—a third of our lives? Teenage girls now are thinking of themselves as people rather than just future wives and mothers. World War

II destroyed the old complacent values and made teenagers question things instead of merely accepting them. We still haven't come to grips with these traumatic changes, but we will in time.

"I was typical—extremely conventional. I was fond of an aunt—not literally an aunt, a wonderful woman who raised me when my mother was sick and my father was in Hollywood—named Mrs. Harold Ober. Her life was running errands in Scarsdale and gardening and providing wonderful meals and being hospitable to dozens of people. It seemed to me the ideal life at the time. Don't misunderstand me, I don't mean that it's still not something to respect or try to attain. But it no longer seems to me the *only* goal a woman should aim for.

"When I thought of the future, I thought of myself surrounded by children, popping popcorn and stringing cranberries like someone out of *The Five Little Peppers and How They Grew*. My concepts about motherhood were romantic, totally unreal. Many of us who were brought up in the solid, comfortable, WASP world I spoke of had dreams of living happily ever after in a picture-book serenity.

"When you lived in this protected world, you had to accept its values. It was tacitly understood that Negroes and Jews were inferior to the rest of us in some vague way. Even if you had your own interior thoughts, you kept quiet about it and didn't make a scene. I remember visiting my mother in Montgomery, Alabama, at sixteen. I announced that I found it shocking the way Negroes there lived. My mother's friends were furious. In those days children of sixteen and even older were supposed to be seen, not heard.

"Obviously I had an advantage, in that I had been raised in many different worlds. My mother was part of the old Southern aristocracy, and many of her friends and relatives were sort of upper-class Tennessee Williams characters. But I was brought up partly in the North and partly in Europe. I had seen enough contrasts to be aware of the obvious inequities.

"Now if a teenager were to walk into a room of staunch, old-line Southerners and take such a view, no one would blink an eye. They might be exasperated, but they wouldn't be shocked. Then it was as if a child today announced she'd become a citizen of Communist China. If I'd been a Southern girl I might have been strung up."

Mrs. Lanahan paused abruptly, then leaned forward. "No, I'm not sure. I probably would have left the South. That's what people generally do if they're unhappy with a situation. You can't fight battles alone, without allies, especially at sixteen.

"I remember another incident down South. I had gone to North Carolina to visit my mother who was in a hospital in Asheville. We were on a bus going to a little place called Blowing Rock. The bus driver made some colored people move back and stand up even though there were loads of seats in the white section. It enraged me so, I got up and moved to the back of the bus to stand with them. My mother stayed where she was and then finally came back and said to me, 'I agree with you, it's awful, but *please* don't do this. You just can't.' I burst into tears and demanded to be let out. Then I stood by the side of the road and waited for the next bus.

"Of course, it didn't prove a thing. Everyone simply thought I was crazy, including the colored people. They didn't know why I was doing it. There wasn't any visible civil rights movement then. I was just a distraught girl behaving badly and my pathetic gesture had absolutely no meaning. If my mother had been younger, she might have felt as I did, but she was of a generation which didn't dare question, let alone challenge. One beauty of today is that kids *can* protest and make it meaningful. They can prove things. In my day, young people had no real voice.

"Several girls only a few years older than I became communists—the Spanish Civil War was what inspired them—and for a while it was fashionable for Vassar girls to go to cell meetings in Poughkeepsie. By the time I got to Vassar the movement was almost over. World events play the largest part in shaping the opinions and ideals of young people. Maybe you're right, after all, about generations occurring every three or four years. Whatever occurs when you are ripe for molding affects your viewpoint ever after.

"We were wildly in love with Franklin Roosevelt, an affection which later transferred itself to Adlai Stevenson, but this was not popular in upper middle-class circles. We kept quiet about it. That's another example of something that just wasn't done: you didn't, in my sixteen-year-old world, admit to being a Democrat, which then meant 'socialist,' roughly translated. FDR was considered a 'traitor to his class.' Can you imagine that expression being used today?

"My four children have political thoughts of their own. They seem to be Democrats, but this has little to do with the fact that their parents are. A teenager who admitted today to being totally influenced by his parents' views would be regarded as square. The trend is to think for yourself, and young people are not viewed with alarm if they have an unorthodox view. On the contrary, their opinions count for something. That may be partly because there are so many of them.

"I shudder to think how immature I was at sixteen. The average sixteen-year-old then was equivalent to a twelve-year-old today. Most twelve-year-olds don't worry much about the future beyond tomorrow, and that's about what I was like. I worried about which boy had written me a letter to an extent which was babyish beyond belief. Come to think of it, I'm not sure young people have changed totally in that particular respect, but they are less silly.

"My concepts for the future were equally infantile. Besides wanting to have the perfect *Little Women* family, I dreamed of composing popular music. The trouble was that I had no idea of what it meant to prepare for a professional career. I just envisioned myself as the famous and witty writer of musical comedies and that was the extent of it. I never seriously considered what to do to make the dream a reality. Few teenagers today would be so naive.

"That's the trouble with getting things for nothing; you come to expect that you always will. I was admitted to Vassar with grades my children couldn't get through high school with. In those days, if you lived in a privileged group, you didn't have to worry about getting into good schools and colleges as long as you had passing marks.

"Nobody today takes getting into college for granted. From the time kids are fifteen, they're under tremendous pressure, which is hard on some. But for serious students who really want to buckle down, it's a good thing. The high-priced education which used to be lavished on daydreamers like me was an utter waste in terms of time and money.

"It is important for sixteen-year-olds to begin preparing for life. There is no substitute for a woman's having a profession and good work habits to go with it. I was twenty-five and a reporter for *The New Yorker* magazine—I never would have been hired except for the war—before I learned how to work. Today the little woman who used to sit at home with the diapers and the dishes waiting for hubby to come home is fast becoming frustrated. By about fourteen, children no longer require all your time and energy, and you really shouldn't interfere too much. So if you've planned your whole life from twenty on until your death around child-rearing, you're left with a large block of terribly empty years. Some friends of mine are already feeling lost and bored, because volunteer work is not always the answer, unless you treat it professionally.

"Our concept of monogamy is not working out too well. The girl who meets her true love in her teens and stays in love with him always is the exception. No girl can ignore the importance of preparing for a career. Even if her marriage is one of the rare, really happy ones, she will enjoy it more if she has independence and a life of her own.

"I'm anxious for my oldest daughter, who has a talent for painting, cartooning and sketching, to pursue it, not to let it go to waste. I care a lot about teenagers, because I have four children ranging in age from fifteen to twenty-one, a pretty composite picture of the new younger generation."

When I asked why she thought the modern girl seemed more mature than her counterpart thirty years ago, she answered: "It's partly the change in reading matter. When I was sixteen, we were still pretty much stuck with *Moby Dick* and *Silas Marner, The Mill on the Floss* and Thackeray and Dickens. Dickens! If he had known children would have to struggle through the magazine serials he dragged out because he was paid by the word, I'm sure he would gladly have cut and edited his novels himself. The *endlessness* of *Great Expectations*. Of course, those classics are worthy of being sampled, but there's really not much a modern young person can iden-tify with. Most of it seems so distant. The only classic I loved at sixteen was Samuel Butler's *The Way of All Flesh*.

"The book of my age, the book we gobbled up ecstatically, was Margaret Mitchell's *Gone with the Wind*. We were all instant Scarlett O'Hara's. How we drank that book in.

"It wasn't until a little later, at about eighteen when I read *Dorian Grey* by Oscar Wilde, that I began to read good books for pleasure. Then I discovered *Of Human Bondage* and other modern books. In those days, the school curriculum tended to make reading a drudgery. Oh, how I hated *Moby Dick!* In some high schools now, they even teach my father. He would have been banned in my day as being scandalous, he, of all people.

"Poetry was something else again. I had problems with poetry for personal reasons. It was one of the few things I rebelled against at sixteen. As a child, my father made me memorize so much poetry I began to dislike it. From seven on he forced me to memorize poems by Keats, Shelley, Thomas Gray, Coleridge. I was fed up with it by the time I got to Vassar and have never been able to enjoy it—a loss maybe I'll make up when I'm sitting on the front porch of a *pension* in Florence in my old age.

"What excited our romanticism most in those days was Fred Astaire and Ginger Rogers in those glorious movies. Our whole little group went to see *Top Hat* seven times, saying the lines with actors which infuriated the people sitting near us. Astaire and Rogers seemed the epitome of grace and beauty, all that we wanted to be. Our other great craze was bandleaders— Benny Goodman and especially Glenn Miller. We used to drive all the way from Baltimore to York, Pennsylvania, to hear them. That was our idea of true adventure, to drive a hundred miles to those huge dance halls that used to exist just for kids our age. It was a very romantic time. Big bands don't go on the road any more as they did then, I don't know why.

"I was too pleased by the music of Cole Porter, Jerome Kern, and Irving Berlin to be attracted to classical music at sixteen.

Later, during the war when I was living with the Harold Obers, I learned to love it. They listened to WQXR, New York's good music station, all the time, and gradually I began to learn something about symphonies and operas.

"My children have many friends in rock 'n roll bands, and they listen to that noise endlessly, just as I sat with mouth open and drank in show tunes. But I do think today's teenagers are being cheated of a lot of genuine musical pleasure. Rock 'n roll obviously doesn't take the same skill and knowledge to write or perform as, say, 'I Get a Kick Out of You.' There is no lyric today worth listening to, or if there is a lyric, it's completely lost in the racket. Teenagers no longer buy scores and memorize music the way we did. The modern stuff is alluring and fun to dance to, and it's healthy—you have to jump up and down to it, and you use up a lot of energy—but a lot of it is wordless noise. The last really good music I remember the children listening to was from *West Side Story*."

Mrs. Lanahan's maid came in to say that *The Washington Post* was on the phone. "I'd better take that one," she said. "My column is due today." When she returned she was smiling and crossed the room with a jaunty walk. "This week's column is about a teenage hangout, and that call reminded me of something very important: the obsolescence of the adolescent male. I think it is one of our most important problems these days. Let me try to explain. In the old days there was a necessity for boys. They were needed to bring in wood, to feed the animals, to do the farming, and in the cities to tend stores, load boats, help with essential chores. Since World War II, there's been less and less for them to do. If every American boy between twelve and eighteen was sent to Australia tomorrow, we would not suffer economically.

"What do parents ask boys to do nowadays? You can say,

'Now dear, Saturday I'd like you to wash the car,' but the job can be done better and more cheaply at the car-wash. You can ask him to mow the lawn, but generally you have a small lawn, and your son can do the job in fifteen minutes with a new electric lawnmower. If you have a big lawn, why should you ask your son to mow it? Obviously, you can afford to pay someone else. He knows that his services aren't necessary, that you can easily exist without his help.

"Because of electricity and automation, there are few physical functions the middle-class boy must perform today. Therefore, getting back to modern music, perhaps it's nature's way of helping boys adjust to the sedentary life they're asked to lead—sitting in a classroom studying all the time. One way to burn up energy is dancing.

"Most parents are bewildered about what to do with their teenage sons. You find an occasional boy with a newspaper route, but often even that's done with the parent driving the boy around the block to make his rounds.

"As a result, I think, you have the teenage gangs, the restlessness, and to some extent violence. They have to have a way to let out their high spirits, and we don't do enough to help them. Three out of the four major race riots last summer started because there were no swimming pools in the neighborhood. The kids were fooling around with the fire hydrants, trying to turn them on. We haven't attacked this problem seriously enough. Where communities have mobilized boys into a sort of cleanup and recreation corps, it's been a huge success. They love responsibility. Otherwise, the 'devil makes work for idle hands'—my grandmother's favorite motto.

"Girls survive somehow. They are always expending their energies on other objects—dolls, animals, other people. They have basically the same preoccupations they always did. Baby-sitting hasn't been automated, for instance. But boys suffer from having all that ego and energy trapped within them until it has to come out, and then when they get in trouble, everybody's surprised and furious.

"What can we do about this? First, the world must take notice and agree that this is a problem. I'm sure there are brilliant people with Ph.D.'s all over the country trying to find solutions to it now.

"My only suggestions would be the obvious ones—swimming pools in every neighborhood, organizations into community services and so forth. What the long-range answer is, I don't know. Even those who can afford to send their sons to expensive schools, with football fields and skating rinks and all the trimmings, still find it difficult; the boys still come home for vacations and slink down on their spines to watch television and do nothing.

"There was the same sort of restlessness in the air just before World War II. I pray a third world war won't be the solution. It's not impossible. Nature has a way of taking care of these problems. It's a terrifying thought, but wars do seem to follow on the heels of times like these, times when young people don't seem to know where they're going. I hope we're smart enough to prevent it.

"As long as I'm on my soapbox, I might as well get in a crack about television, too. The dullness of my generation's reading matter in school was nothing compared to the monster we've given birth to in television. Most people realize it, talk about it, fume about it, and nothing gets done. I don't think it's ever going to get any better until parents demand that the government take a hand.

"Television has influenced these kids' lives too much, and once again it's the boys who are being affected. Violence has always been the little-boy tradition. We give little boys guns and little girls dolls, a death-symbol for the boy and a life-symbol for the girl. What irony. If we conducted a poll, we would find the majority of American people don't want this continuous flow of crime and violence on TV. They'd welcome a certain amount of government control over television. Then someone could say, 'All right, you can have one hour of crime and shooting on each station every day, and that's all.' In England, which does have a government-controlled network, it's an absolute joy to watch the telly.

"Of course young people would complain. They've been force-fed this junk from the time they were old enough to watch TV. Take the boy who lined five women up in the hairdressing shop and shot them. Obviously, there was TV influence here. I wish the Texas murderer who shot from the tower hadn't been killed. We could have put him under obser-vation and really studied him. I'll bet television was the single biggest influence in his life.

"At least nobody has managed to make a hero of Lee Harvey Oswald. Teenagers just accept the fact that Kennedy was shot and killed because they live in such a climate of violence it seems almost natural. Oh, they're horrified and saddened and they grieve. It will probably take a number of years to deter-mine just how greatly his death has affected them, but I don't think they are as shocked by his assassination as children of another age would have been.

"Of course, there are wonderful advantages to being a teen-ager today. There is such opportunity for young people to try new things, to become educated as never before, to find them-selves on their own terms—what many members of my genera-tion were too timid to do. Parents today are more enlightened than they were when I was sixteen. They've learned that you must respect young people as individuals rather than forcing them into molds you've preconceived for them. You must let your children make some of their own mistakes instead of simply handing down your own.

"Many of the friends I had when I was sixteen are proof of how tragic it is to try to be what you're not. They grew up struggling to conform to the image their parents had ordained for them, and many of them have fallen by the wayside in this respect—nervous breakdowns, broken lives. Perhaps the point I'm making is that we were happier at sixteen than our children are—ignorance is bliss—but we paid a price for this innocence. We were sheltered and protected and our decisions were made for us, so that when the time came to face up to reality later on, many of us hadn't the ability to cope.

"Teenagers today make their own decisions, which can be very painful. It's always difficult. They're not as carefree or as oblivious of the world around them as we were, quite the opposite. They grow up faster and face a lot of problems precisely because they aren't held down. For instance, girls from sixteen on must decide what they're going to do with all the sexual freedom which is suddenly thrust on them, unheard of when I was that age. They haven't got God, parents or even society setting down clear-cut rules.

"What I'm really trying to say is that you always pay for everything. My generation paid later on for the snug little unseeing world we inhabited then. My children's generation is paying as they go along for the freedom and individuality they've been granted. I think in the long run it will work out better for them. Seeing things as they are, rather than through a pair of leftover Victorian eyeglasses, is more trying for both children and parents, but today's kids will be more apt to make sensible decisions than my generation was."

Oliver Baker

Marianne Moore

*When Marianne Moore won the Pulitzer Prize, the National
Book Award, the Bollingen Prize and, to top it off, the Gold
Medal for Poetry of the National Institute of Arts and Letters
—all in 1952—she became something of a celebrity. Miss Moore
had not particularly wanted to become a celebrity, but, charac-
teristically, she found her new reputation fascinating. She
enjoyed attending Truman Capote's masked ball at the Plaza
Hotel in 1966. She enjoyed discussing poetry with Cassius
Clay. And she enjoyed wearing a black velvet tricorne designed*

especially for her in a hat-modeling parade in Manhattan's garment district. ("I like the tricorne shape because it conceals defects of the head," she once explained to a newspaper reporter.) Miss Moore, now seventy-nine years old, is less eccentric than direct. She seems incapable of equivocation.

Miss Moore was born in Saint Louis, where she was raised mainly by her mother and her maternal grandfather, a Presbyterian minister. Upon moving with her mother and older brother to Carlisle, Pennsylvania, she attended the Metzger Institute, where her mother taught English. The three of them —Marianne, her brother John, and her mother, Mrs. Mary Warner Moore—were extraordinarily close.

In 1905, Miss Moore entered Bryn Mawr College. There, she later said, "Most of my time was spent in the biology laboratory despite my interest in English language courses, for which I seemed not to have an aptitude." After graduating from Bryn Mawr, Miss Moore taught typing, shorthand and bookkeeping for four years at the Carlisle Indian School, run by the federal government. One of her students was Jim Thorpe, who became the most famous athlete of his day.

Despite her difficulties with college English courses, some of Miss Moore's poems were printed in student publications at Bryn Mawr. In 1915, when she was twenty-eight, her poems were first printed in Egoist, *a magazine published by the British imagists, and* Poetry, *run by Harriet Monroe in Chicago. Miss Moore's first collection,* Poems, *appeared in 1921. It came as a surprise to her: two other* Egoist *poets had compiled and published the collection as a present.*

Two years before, Miss Moore and her mother had moved to New York City. They settled in a Greenwich Village basement apartment, and, in 1921, Miss Moore began working at the local branch of the New York Public Library while con-

tinuing to write poetry. In 1924, Miss Moore's second book of poetry, Observations, *won the* Dial *award, granted by one of the best avant-garde magazines of the Twenties.*

The next year Miss Moore became acting editor of The Dial. *During her editorship, the magazine published Yeats, Cummings, Williams, Eliot, Gorky, Lawrence, and many other leading writers, as well as art by Picasso and Stuart Davis. Miss Moore, an unfrivolous lady who lived quietly with her mother, had become a leading figure in the nation's intellectual life. That fact did little to change the style of her own life.*

In 1929, with members of the Dial *staff no longer living adjacent to the office, it was decided to discontinue the magazine. Miss Moore and her mother then moved to Brooklyn. They found an apartment in the Clinton Hill section, because Miss Moore's brother, a United States Navy chaplain, was then stationed nearby at the Brooklyn Navy Yard. Miss Moore lived in this apartment until 1966, when she returned to Greenwich Village.*

There, Miss Moore continues to write poetry—when she is not chatting with the corner butcher, watching baseball, or attending botany lectures at the Brooklyn Museum. She recently published another collection of poems, Tell Me, Tell Me: Granite, Steel and Other Topics *(1966), on subjects as various as Leonardo da Vinci, cancer researchers, Yogi Berra and the arctic musk ox.*

Miss Moore's poetry is characterized by careful attention to the particular. Her poems were once likened to "definitions, encyclopedia articles set to music." They have been often praised for restraint and wit, and T. S. Eliot termed them "part of the small body of durable poetry written in our time . . . in which original sensibility and alert intelligence and deep feeling have been engaged in maintaining the life of the English language."

Miss Moore remains close to her brother and often sees his daughters. But, as always, she frequently likes to be alone. When she is in the proper mood—"humility, concentration, and gusto," as she once called it—she feels like "a cat in the basket with the lid on" or "a badger under a hedge of poison ivy." In that mood, she writes poetry.

Marianne Moore

AFTER she had greeted me Miss Moore lit three lights, which made the sturdy arrangement of the room and her own small figure more clear. She wore a dark skirt and a white blouse with a half-inch black ribbon tied in a bow at the collar. Turning her back for a moment to wind an old-fashioned clock, she said, "I want this clock to go, but it won't go. I overwound it."

Miss Moore has many fine antiques in her Greenwich Village apartment, and she told me the history of one when I asked, "As a child, did you live in a town?"

"Always have," Miss Moore said. "But I spent summers on a farm. That highboy was built from the walnut trees on a farm called Locust Hill in Pennsylvania. Since it belonged to Margaret Boyd, it has her initials inlaid in the top center drawer."

At the far end of Miss Moore's living room are two square windows which provide a pleasant view of the quiet street on which she lives. The curtains at the windows are Union blue.

"My grandfather," said Miss Moore, "was a Presbyterian minister and was present during the Battle of Gettysburg. He was a pastor there, and his wife, my grandmother, died of typhoid fever as a result of the battle, since conditions in Gettysburg were very unwholesome.

"My brother was born in Massachusetts; I, in Missouri. As young children we lived with my aunt and grandfather, my grandfather being pastor of a Presbyterian church in Kirkwood, Missouri. He had a little white manse with a porch and about five white buildings surrounding it.

"There were oak trees and bluejays in the churchyard. An aunt had sent me a little alligator as a pet, and we had numerous kittens. There were flowers along the fence between our yard and the adjoining one, with crimson roses and white clematis along the fence which separated the two yards—in the autumn, chrysanthemums—and there was spatterdock in tubs by the back door.

"We children attended a kindergarten and carried a small market basket holding an orange and butter-thin biscuits.

"We then went to live in Pennsylvania. My brother attended high school, and I, Metzger Institute. My mother taught English there. She prepared me for Bryn Mawr and spoiled me badly.

"I was diffident when I was sixteen, intimidated by sleigh rides, barn dances and such parties. I was interested in animals and sports, and after school I read books like *Captains Courageous* and *Stories Mother Nature Told Her Children, For Freedom's Cause* and one about Scotland. I was always reading or preparing lessons. I was over-anxious when sixteen. I'd be uncertain whether I'd pass this or that subject. My main thought was to know English and French—I'd read Carlyle. But I couldn't take French at Metzger and I couldn't take

English, not elective, that is, so I was badly disappointed. Then later on I wanted very much to go to Bryn Mawr. I did go there. I was one of two girls in the Latin course, the only girl in French.

"I also took piano lessons, but I've forgotten it by now. I'm very fond of music. I even took singing lessons—not because I could sing, because I could *not*. I had a very dutiful teacher. She was really a precisionist and did me a lot of good. We had chapel and had to sing 'Onward, Christian Soldiers.' I used to sing it like this: 'Onward, Christian Sold-i-e-rs.' My teacher said, 'You must never do that. Cut the long note out.' I admired that. She was articulate.

"I never cared much for poetry then, though I did read the classics—Spenser, Tennyson, the early English poets. I was plagued, of course, by having to master subjects to get into college. There wasn't the pressure of today, but I wanted to. People said to me, 'Why don't you go to Dickinson College? It's coeducational, and you and your brother can both go.' But I had met some graduates of Bryn Mawr who seemed to me very talented and unusual. I thought I'd like to be like them.

"When I got there, the teams of girls were coming up from the athletic field and were far from beautiful. Their hair hung down over their faces, their hockey skirts were dragging. Otherwise we wore velveteen. There were different colors for each class—yellow, blue, darker blue, green and red. The color of my class was red. We made up a song:

> Ruber ruber ruber rex
> DCCICIX

Later on, I gave a course in Contemporary Poetry there, in 1953, second semester.

"My brother went to Yale. He was very self-reliant. I was

homesick, very. I'd never been anywhere. Oh, to Boston, and before I was in college my mother took us to Florida to see historic sites, the Fountain of Eternal Youth, and the compositions of rock and shell walls characteristic of old towns in Florida. I heard about Pizarro and Ponce de Leon and saw a Spanish dungeon. The prisoners were lowered into the prison through a high window; food was let down to them. They were never released."

I asked Miss Moore how she had spent her time when she was sixteen.

"I was always reading then," she answered. "I read Dickens from one end to the other; I was getting ready for college. When I was in college, Kipling and Henry James. But more to the point, *now* I am reading Augustus Buell's *Life of John Paul Jones,* from which I am learning a great deal. He is someone who can write.

"Now I regret that I didn't study chemistry and Greek in college. But I didn't. When I was sixteen, I felt as old and decisive as when I was fifty or sixty. Especially when I was fifteen to twenty, I rarely listened to reason. I think you should be open-minded and as grateful to people as you can be. We should judge ourselves by the least that we are, and judge others by the most that they are. Rate other people as high as we can.

"People ask me, 'How do you think of things to write about?' I don't. *They* think of *me.* They become *irresistible.* I was looking at my little book, the one just out:

> Tell me, tell me
> where there might be a refuge for me
> from egocentricity.

I would say, 'Don't think about yourself from morning to night.' As for egotism, paranoia and putting pressure on others, most people say you have to be inconsiderate or you won't get anywhere. I've always felt that pushiness and pushy people are obnoxious."

I asked Miss Moore how she would define "growing up," and she answered: "To me, growing up means being able to change from a fixed opinion. When you become liberalized in your judgment, then you are growing up. You are grown up when you make a sacrifice on behalf of another person and don't call it a sacrifice. I do not like slacks on women, let's say. But there's something to be said for them. I was amazed when a friend of mine and I went to the country together. She had on canvas britches. I thought, 'Maybe she ought to wear a skirt.' But I changed my mind—there were brambles, blackberries and wire to surmount. As *Punch* said, 'How do you know whether our "striplings" are boys or girls?' Don't belittle yourself. Change or be at home with yourself. If you fail, better have it that way.

"I like to read. I like *The Glory of Their Times* by Lawrence Ritter, a baseball book about early players. If I begin one of these accounts, I just have to read right on to the end. It was the same with the *Life of Wilkie Collins* by Kennett Robinson. (Collins wrote *The Moonstone* and *The Woman in White*.) Sometimes people ask me which I like best of the ballplayers now playing. I could give a guess, but I do not like preferences, comparisons.

"I am also asked, 'What do you see in animals?' They are not self-conscious, are consummately graceful and knowing sometimes. Ted Atkinson, the jockey, said about Tom Fool, 'He was the most intelligent horse I ever rode.' That interests me.

"I like anything connected with horses. Have you seen the Horse Show at Madison Square Garden? And I like the theater, though I haven't been to a play for some time. What I really like is to be out in the open air, play tennis, go sailing. I have my trapeze, but neglect it. I didn't use to.

"I lived in Brooklyn until recently. We used to have there, at the Brooklyn Institute, the cream of the museum experts, Dr. Bailey, Dr. Ripley and others. I took notes on what they said about penguins, cormorants, ducks." She went on to name more birds than I can enumerate. References to birds and animals are frequent in her poetry, too; a random glance at the table of contents of her *Collected Poems* shows: "The Jerboa," "No Swan So Fine," "The Frigate Pelican," "The Buffalo," "The Monkeys," "Bird-Witted," "The Wood-Weasel," "Sea Unicorns and Land Unicorns," "An Octopus" and "To the Peacock of France."

Miss Moore described some aspects of her own writing with characteristic modesty: "As I said to John Mason Brown at the National Book Awards, when he asked, 'What would you say about your writing?' 'Well, the only reason for calling it poetry is there is no other category in which to put it.' That's true, I say it still. So if someone wants to write, I would say, 'By all means, do. Nothing could be better if you don't expect everything to be a masterpiece.'

"I notice that most new writers remind us of other writers. Once at Sarah Lawrence College, R. P. Blackmur said to a man, 'I see that you don't agree with me.' The man said, 'I don't read poetry—only read Shakespeare and Dante.' Mr. Blackmur said, 'We don't come in that big size.'

"I don't like verse that is self-conscious and haughty. I think we ought to be natural. And it always puts me off when I come on the reversed order of words. But one piece I was fascinated by begins:

> No man may him hyde
> From Deth holow-eyed.

"Accents. Rhythm was my whole interest in verse in the beginning. But strive for the natural. As you know, you're not supposed to rhyme an *acc*ented and an *un*accented syllable. Well, the *Fables* of La Fontaine *inebriated* me by the way in which La Fontaine broke rules. I hadn't even read him before I translated his *Fables*.

"Someone once said to me, 'You must be a very brave person because you always do what you are afraid of doing.' I was very pleased because I am somewhat 'schizoid.' But why not? Why expose myself? Why can't I be private?

"Last evening I spent an hour and a half just opening my letters. In the morning I look at them. Sometimes in the past I didn't eat until about noon, I was so determined to get my mail answered. Now I eat as soon as I wake up—cereal, fruit juice. If there is a really urgent letter, I answer it first. Someone may be in a hurry for a book for Christmas and wants it signed: 'Could you let me have it before Christmas?' I say, 'If you accompany it with a jiffy bag, I'll do it.' At present, though, my signature is rather scratchy.

"Well, I think it's natural for people who like a thing to want to know all they can about the author. I wanted very much, once, to meet Thomas Hardy. But nothing would induce me to go to Max Gate [his home in England] and say, 'I just want to speak to you.' In proportion as you value a person, you ought to protect the person.

"What has made most impression on me in recent years was going to Venice and Greece. And the next year going to Cornwall and Ireland, to Belfast, North Ireland, then South Ireland. Everything I had read in books came to life. Have you been to Greece, seen the olive trees and the goats, and the magpies flitting and hopping? Then in England, that grayish misty countryside and the hills. And going to battlefields in

Greece. I brought home some laurel from Marathon. I keep it
in this box made of olive wood. I even visited the olive tree
under which Plato sat, a high excitement. I wish I could go
again, to see the real and tangible Discobolus and various other
statues reproduced, as it were, forever, the Calf-bearer, the
Gladiator, Laocoön. And then the Acropolis!

"I was also at a little folk museum at Piraeus. We ate octopus
and little clams by the waterside. Well, I brought home four or
five, they were so beautifully formed. I wanted to go up
Santorini on a donkey, and did. Then I was determined to buy
me a donkey bell, but the driver couldn't understand English. I
said, 'You promised to get me one, I must have it!'—and he cut
the bell right off the donkey. I gave him about twice what he
wanted for it, and I do have much amusement from it.

"I have it, and a little walrus-ivory ox carved by an Eskimo
in Alaska, Ken Henrickson . . .

"John J. Teal, Jr., is raising musk ox on his farm in Vermont.
He showed a film of musk ox at Abercrombie's in their top
story. You could sit in a window seat or a chair and see this
film. It showed how they captured an ox under great difficulties. Well, the plane companies aren't allowed to carry
animals, but thought a few muskrats might be permitted. He
faced them with enormous creatures weighing two or three
hundred pounds. They are still growing. Let us hope they
won't multiply till they have to be thinned out. They are very
gentle animals and produce more wool than Australian cashmere rams do. You can make seven men's suits out of the wool
of one ram, can shear and spin oxdown. Mr. Teal wrote an
article, 'Golden Fleece of the Arctic,' from which I derived one
of my poems. When my brother heard the poem, he said, 'It
sounds just like an advertisement.'

" 'Well,' I said, 'it is.' "

A few more tales and it was late afternoon. Miss Moore said, "I think you will have to leave now." She accompanied me to the door through a small foyer and paused a moment. "But you should not make me seem dogmatic. I'm tentative," she said.

Ruth Fuller, M.D.

Ruth Fuller was born in 1937 in a small town in upstate New York. She grew up in Queens, a borough of New York City. By her senior year at Newtown High School—where she was an excellent student in chemistry, physics and mathematics—she was sure she wanted a career in one of the applied sciences.

[232]

She took a bachelor's degree in chemistry at Howard University, Washington, D.C., and went on to medical school at Downstate Medical Center in Brooklyn, New York. Concentrating on the study of psychiatry, she interned and served a two years residency in psychiatry at Kings County Hospital in Brooklyn. Then, "because I like kids," she elected to become a child psychiatrist, and trained in this sub-specialty for another two years at Kings.

Currently Dr. Fuller works in various capacities at two mental health clinics. One is a hospital-affiliated Manhattan clinic; the other, part of a community health center in the Bronx. She instructs social workers and others who are concerned with children, conducts group and private therapy, and is on call for emergency cases. She also has a private practice, working in her office at home.

In 1961, Dr. Fuller married Courtney Callender, now Director of Community Relations for the New York City Parks Department. They met while she was an undergraduate at Howard.

Ruth Fuller, M.D.

THE USUAL PICTURE of medical school is that you work from dawn to dawn with no reward, that it is all drudgery. It's not so. It *is* hard work, the hours *are* long. And when you look at your textbooks you wonder how you went through all of them. 'Did I really learn all that?' you ask yourself. The truth is, you were carried through by a kind of *taste* for learning that has to be present when you are applying yourself in any field."

Dr. Ruth Fuller was talking in the living room of the apartment where she and her husband live on the Upper West Side of Manhattan. Her manner is matter-of-fact and direct, but her voice is soft and feminine. We sat together on a red plush sofa. A small woman with short-cropped hair that sets off a delicately shaped head, she was wearing a brightly colored print hostess gown. "When you called to ask for an interview," she said at one point, "I was more worried about what to wear than about what I'd say."

The apartment is overflowing and lively. One corner is

occupied by a venerable roll-top desk, bookshelves and a giant bulletin board. The window sills are full of odd-shaped plants and a pierced-brass temple lamp. There is a round oak table with a Tiffany lamp shade over it, and paintings by children are on two walls. On the bulletin board a giant poster announces a build-your-own-house party, or what New Yorkers call a "Hoving Happening," to be held in Central Park.

I was impressed by her calmness whether she was talking or listening. She is a receptive, professional listener and sometimes she can make a questioner feel questioned.

"When I turned sixteen," she continued, "I was a senior at Newtown High School in Queens, New York. My birthday was just before graduation, as a matter of fact. All I knew about my future at sixteen was that I was headed into the sciences, probably one of the applied sciences, but I wasn't sure which one. I started college the second half of my sixteenth year. That was at Howard University in Washington, D.C. I took a pre-med major, beginning with chemistry and zoology. After college I went on to medical school. I took one careful step at a time.

"There were many influences affecting my decision to become a doctor—teachers, family, people who had attained their goals in life in various professions. The people who were most important to me were interested in me in a very freeing way. They said, 'These are the kinds of things that you might be able to do. Take a look at them and try them on for size and see what fits best.' My parents wanted a life and a kind of work for me that I would enjoy and find rewarding, intellectually stimulating. How I attained it, though, depended on my finding my particular life style. They were willing to let me discover the one that suited me. It was an open-ended approach from everyone. But I think that's truly helpful when you're moving in many, many directions and you're not quite sure which is going to be best. I liked the freedom to be able to experiment a little. I enjoyed that freedom, and I also felt that learning was important, no matter what use I put it to. People believed that I had a talent for something, and it was up to me to find this talent and develop it.

"My first introduction to science came not in high school but in junior high, on a very, very basic level. The work I was given as a ninth-grader was interesting and something quite new to me. My interest grew through high school; the idea of applied science developed somewhat later. Someone in the ninth grade has great difficulty understanding what medical school and the practice of medicine are really like. You know about going to see a doctor, but it's a little difficult to visualize how that doctor got to be who he is. You might have some notion of being a doctor as a senior in high school, but it's very hard to know what it's going to be like eight or ten years from then when you *are* a doctor. Eight to ten years is a long time when you're sixteen. The idea of staying in school 'for the rest of your life' seems forbidding. After all, you think everyone is middle-aged at twenty-five, approaching old age at thirty! But by the first year of college I felt that even though I was studying, I was doing other things, too, and that my life didn't stop because I was a student.

"My high school situation encouraged me a lot. Fortunately, at various points some very, very hopeful and very, very fine teachers took a special interest in me, particularly in giving me guidance. Even though they were teachers, their thoughts were about the student's development first and their subject second. I remember one especially. He was a young man in his thirties who taught English. His great interest was creative writing, but he couldn't teach that because there was an older woman in the department and she had seniority. Still, he made the rather ordinary aspects of English very exciting. He was very intense, as I recall. A little of his passion as an under-graduate had lasted, and he gave it to us. Sometimes he would talk about things of doubtful utility. I remember one day he launched into a long discussion of diction and pronunciation. I think what started it was something about O'Neill's misuse of American idiom; he talked about the difference between British and American English. His point was that it didn't really matter which you used as long as you were consistent. It was really a lecture on precision of language, but the way we got this information, in a discussion that seemed pure play, made me remember what he said long after.

"I asked these teachers all kinds of questions: what is college; what do you do in college; what do you do in graduate school; how does my math class relate to my being in college; what do I have to take if I want to be a physician? Many of these questions seemed large at first, but there were people who had the answers and who wanted to give them to me, and as a result these questions just decreased in size until they were in proportion to the problem. When I moved on through the next level, there were new questions, but I could handle them: what is medical school, what do you do there?

"I suppose I had mixed feelings, though, about asking ques-tions. One feeling is that the question sounds dumb and the reproach might be, 'You mean you're sixteen years old and you haven't figured that out yet?' Or else you think, 'If I wait a little bit, I'll figure it out myself, and then I'll have the satisfaction of knowing that I didn't have to ask anyone.' The mixture of these two things sometimes interferes with the ability to ask at all.

"But my friends and I *were* able to pose these questions and try to find people who could answer them. I think in one way we felt that college and graduate school couldn't be so mysterious because there were people *in* them. And we were competitive, as most kids in groups are. Each of us wanted to be the best informed and have the most novel bit of information. But I think we also felt that group interest was involved, that misinformation could lead us all astray."

Dr. Fuller spoke as if her group of high school friends had been very close. "How had that happened?" I asked.

"I think probably the attraction at first was intellectual," she said. "We were kind of flung together—not by choice but by the Board of Education. Then we got to be friends. We had secrets and we planned social activities for the future. And we most certainly did plan for the very distant future! All these things created a further bond. There must have been eight of us, girls and boys. Within that eight there were groups of two and one group of four and then there were another three or four that were sometimes in the group and sometimes not.

"We were the kind of kids who had part-time jobs after school, usually ones we'd scrounged for ourselves. One girl was manager at a candy store. We didn't know what the manager of a candy store did, but she made it sound real good to the owner, and he hired her. We were always thinking up things to do for people and ways to get paid. We were joiners at school, too; being active in sports was a big thing—you got to take trips.

"We all really cared for each other, and caring and being cared for are crucial at sixteen. The great bursts of creativity and feeling, the sudden sense of being acutely aware that you are you, of an intense need to communicate with someone, and with someone that you feel understands, can sometimes be extremely frustrating and frightening. You begin to wonder, 'Am I the only person in the world that feels this? Am I the only person in the world that experiences this?' And the answer seems to be, 'Yes, I am,' and then you are finally very worried or very lonely. Then you wish for somebody to see what you see, to recognize it and share it with you. But there's a two-way street that develops.You feel the trauma and magic of being able to care about someone and knowing that someone cares about you. Then the world looks much lovelier. Terribly unhappy things do happen, but there's a kind of faith that there are other people who feel the same way. Then you begin to realize that people aren't so unique and that somewhere others like you exist.

"Perhaps the most difficult thing for a sixteen-year-old is when you feel that there is no one, when there's not one friend, no one who is interested. But the energy and feeling-of-being-sixteen have to go somewhere. When I look back, I find that I wrote many lovely things then. I used to write a lot when I was lonely. I could never write that way again.

"I was an only child, but I never felt like one. We had a large, close family of uncles and aunts and cousins. Of course, I couldn't make regular visits to those living on the West Coast but there were enough in the New York area, and even enough in Queens, to give me the feeling that I wasn't exactly alone in the world. Both my parents came from large families and they all migrated north and west out of the Carolinas.

"My mother was—and still is—a seamstress, fitter and designer. She loved me and paid attention to what I said, but she wasn't, in many ways, a very conventional mother. She was interested in my safety and my education, all the things parents are usually interested in, but her approach was often pretty original. One night the group was determined to go to a party in a terrible blizzard. The party was in the far reaches of Queens and our ride had disappeared, of course—he showed a little sense about the weather! At first, Mother just refused to let me go, and painted wild pictures of being stranded all night in the snow. But when we got a substitute ride and were obviously going no matter what, Mother's solution was to go with us. She said it would be better to be lost and cold together. So we took off, and we made it to the party.

"But it was the trip back that was really marvelous. The snow stopped, and a full moon came out. It's hard to find white, unbroken snow in New York, but there it was, beautiful and quiet. It was worth dragging my mother out into a blizzard just to see that. It was a nice evening and I was glad my mother was there. I realized that evening how much, even though I was sixteen, I still needed her, although I would have promptly denied it." She broke off to smile at the cat, Samantha, stalking an imaginary prey across the room. "That cat is shedding in clumps all over the house. I think she has a vitamin deficiency."

Had her parents approved of the close relationship among the group's members? I asked.

"They approved of us," she said, "though I think many parents are quite worried to see such a thing. There is a large potential in such a group—power is an apt word—and it can move in any direction. Until our parents were sure of which way we were going, they worried. Basically, that group experience in adolescence allowed me to move from relationships in my family to relationships with strangers. Sure, many times I excluded my family or my older friends. They didn't always fit into what I thought was important. But this new feeling that we all had for each other was important, too, part of growing up. Now I look back and see what great capacities were stimulated in me, and in my friends, by our relationship, even though sometimes we had to exclude our parents. Our approach

[241]

to each other gave us what I now see as an ability to share. We became accustomed to meeting demands because we were with some very demanding people, but at the same time we received a great deal.

"We had a sense of fun, too, that went along with our intensity. It was really a kind of sobering force; it made the intensity a little less ominous. For example, we were always making up *occasions*. The bigger holidays were taken for granted, so we moved on to the minor ones—ground-hog day was always a good excuse for a dinner. Birthdays were a very big thing, too. Mostly we ate with each other, especially on birthdays. As we got older, even a new recipe was an excuse for a big dinner—we were all interested in cooking. And the ones who were artists or singers would have student shows and recitals.

"Dates were very important to us but we sought the security of the group as well. There were a lot of things we weren't aware of—we saw sex as merely a function of intercourse rather than a concept of sharing and of communication. I think we feared individual dating, and there never seemed to be less than four boys and four girls when we went out. I'd go to a party or a movie on Saturday night with one boy, but by the end of the evening there'd be five or six of us going out for coffee. Or someone would call to say, 'Who are you going to the concert with?' and you'd end up going with four or five others. Of course, I had crushes—sometimes for as long as a month. And then, boom! The scales would be lifted from my eyes and I'd think, 'How could I have been so immature as to take *him* seriously?'

"We were very curious and concerned about sex. It presented a challenge to us, and for some of us it was hard to resist. But there were a lot of things we *were* aware of that made survival more important than meeting this challenge. You know, in eighth grade, even seventh grade, we'd see a friend pregnant at thirteen or so, and only about half aware of how it had happened. We'd see what that did to her life. Of course, if we'd lived in a middle-class or upper-class neighborhood, we might never have seen what happened. But in a working-class environment there aren't enough resources to send a girl away, to arrange for adoption, so the girl stayed home and had the baby and that was that. But we saw the results. She couldn't go to school any more—the schools are more understanding now—and she came to football games with a child who wasn't her kid brother. We found out that none of us were prepared to make those sacrifices. We talked about it a lot, and frequently we saw sex as a question dealing with reality: 'Baby, I've got enough problems without adding *that* one.'"

"What has happened to the group since?" I asked. "Did you all go to college together?"

"No," Dr. Fuller said, "most of us scattered and went to different colleges. Some stayed in the city and a number went out of town, but we'd correspond and meet over the holidays. Now we're all over the country, as far as California and the Midwest, but we still know where we all are, roughly. Most of us were headed for the sciences, though, and several of us have gone into medicine, at least four or five. A couple of others went into research. There was only one who went into the arts, and he made the decision much later. The bulk of us met each other again years afterward and found that we were all going to medical schools in different places.

"Would you like some coffee?" she interrupted herself. "I've found a great new Instant. When I'm working late at night I can't bother with brewing from scratch." She was already halfway to the kitchen. She boiled water, found milk and sugar and filled our cups in what seemed to be one motion. On the way from the stove with the water, she tripped slightly—"I keep telling myself that clumsy people are more endearing," she chuckled.

We began to talk about college. "At Howard I found a new group of friends," she said. "I think people do find each other. Our group in high school had finally expanded to about sixteen people. In college it started out smaller, but even so I rarely found myself completely alone unless I wanted to be. My friends were sensitive enough to know when I wanted a quiet time and to let me have it. We assumed, for example, that meal-times were important, that they were a little bit prolonged and that you never ate alone. You could probably get all of your food down in twelve minutes, but there was an exchange that took place, and this needed time. We picked a place for lunch, for dinner, for Sunday brunch. On Sundays we explored the city. We'd look at a guidebook and we'd go someplace. So we saw all of Washington, which I think is a beautiful city. We talked to each other and ran around all weekend and went back to work on Monday.

"I suppose that in one way I was unusual. I wasn't just a hard-working kid who could make it through college and medical school and end up fairly successful. I had a close group of friends in high school and developed another good group in college—one led to the other, most certainly—so I was never afraid my friends would disappear because I was off studying for an exam. I could just relax and do my work. That way I enjoyed school very much.

"There was no fear that we were missing something— marriage, for instance. I think the push to get married at the end of college or at the end of high school varies from group to group. In some circles if you get to the graduation line in college and you are not engaged, you've failed your second major and you've done a terrible thing—you may have missed your golden opportunity. This feeling is very strong, sometimes based on stories about the experience of a very dear family friend, now sixty-two years old, who didn't get engaged in college and found no other eligible man, ever. I heard this story, but I didn't feel it. Although it is true that college provides a marvelous opportunity for meeting future mates, in my own case I waited to be married till long after college. Marriage wasn't an issue for me in college because my friends and I had great mobility, both physical and emotional. Most certainly the then boys-becoming-men were very social minded and very interested in girlfriends. They thought about the future and about marriage. If they were financially able, some of them did marry and then finished college and went on to medical school. The other friends wanted to finish college and medical school first, and this is what they did. Whichever way we chose to combine our marriage and our professional life, there was no great deprivation to any of us.

"I never felt more deprived in attending school than anyone would who is open and curious about life. There are always choices that have to be made. There *are* sacrifices, there have to be. You can't go to all the parties; you may have to turn down a date for the movies or the theater that you've been trying to maneuver for several weeks because it comes up the night before finals. But you keep in mind that you have to give up some things in this world.

"On the other hand, I think the necessity for putting in long hours of work at college is exaggerated so that students won't get the idea that college is all fun, that you only have to show up with your books two or three times a semester. Of course, you won't get much out of college doing that. Then, too, parents have the memory of college as hard work rather than fun. They regard the fun aspect as a frivolous, silly kind of thing because the purpose of college, to them, is to study very hard and find yourself at the end ready for a career. Parents are naturally concerned about a teenaged boy or girl; they are worried about preparing him to *do* something.

"But there can be a balance between work and fun, and in the first year of college there's a great deal of help in finding it. Seniors are appointed to guide and counsel freshmen, and other people help with setting up a program. The second year is harder, because then the student is left more on his own. The seniors seem to disappear; they're more concerned with the new group of freshmen and getting them started. And by the end of the second year, when you're supposed to declare your major and commit yourself to a field of study, you may not be quite sure what you want to do.

"So the third and fourth years are probably more fun because you finally filled out the card that says, 'I am going to major in this or that.' I was a chemistry major, and knew it early. But if you decide you will make up your mind in your senior year and that you'll just be in college to get an education and see what you can learn, you get pretty anxious. The goal that a freshman had at sixteen or eighteen can change completely by the time he graduates at twenty-one or twenty-two.

"I was just twenty when I finished college, and then I went to medical school in Brooklyn—Downstate Medical Center; it's part of the State University. I did all of my training there, internship at an affiliated hospital, and residency at the largest affiliate—Kings County Hospital. My training at Kings County was in psychiatry. To be a psychiatrist, you need a minimum of three years' training. My field, child psychiatry, is a sub-specialty and requires two years of training after the two years in general psychiatry. Psychoanalysis also begins with training in general psychiatry, then goes on to another program of at least four years. All psychiatric specialties begin from the same starting point and then diverge."

I asked Dr. Fuller why child psychiatry had appealed to her. She raised her eyebrows in surprise, as if it were the most obvious choice in the world.

"That's easy, because there's really only one answer possible: I like kids. They're flexible and funny and growing, and to deal with them you have to be just as flexible as they are. If you overhear a conversation about sex, for instance: Suzie may be telling Betsy that babies are born because mothers eat some horrendous mixture of things, and Betsy will interrupt five times: 'You're crazy,' 'Suzie, you've got it all wrong,' 'No, Suzie.' You might decide that Betsy was totally enlightened unless you waited until the end, when Betsy is likely to say, 'I *told* you you had it all wrong. You forgot the *pumpkin* seed.'

"You have to be ready for these things, ready to answer the questions they ask. It's a funny business, just listening and responding. You'd be surprised how few parents ever learn just to listen.

"I think the medical school you attend plays a large role in determining the number of students who go into psychiatry. If it's introduced as a crucial part of the medical program— viewing the patient as a whole person with feelings and problems and strengths and weaknesses—psychiatry becomes as much a part of making an adequate assessment of a person's health as listening to his heart. The interest in psychiatry varies, depending on what section of the country you're in. It also depends on the amount of exposure to it you get in the medical schools. My exposure began early with a basic introduction in the first year, and by the third we spent time working in the psychiatric service. In some schools there is little or no emphasis on psychiatry and exposure comes much later. At a school like that I would probably have been much better acquainted with general medicine or pediatrics or radiology.

"Of course, here in New York there is special interest in psychiatric training because there is a great shortage of psychiatrists. There are so many community health programs here that there are just not enough psychiatrists to staff the centers. The development of psychiatry seems to move along with that of cities. Fifty miles outside of New York it would be quite different, and in some states psychiatrists are very rare.

"But for any medical specialty, energy and confidence are what count in the long run. I work now at a clinic and at a health center, and I have a private practice. It's hard work, and the hours aren't short, but I guess after eight or ten years you get used to it. The energy is there, and so is the need to put it to use."

I asked Dr. Fuller how being a Negro had affected her—socially, professionally, emotionally.

"Sometimes it's meant a lot, sometimes not so much." She grinned at her own noncommittal answer, then went on. "That is a very hard question to answer since I've never known what it's like not to be a Negro. Sometimes being a Negro affects your life more intensely than it does at other times, but being Negro always means being different from being white or purple or green. The opportunities that existed for me were different than they would have been had I been white, for instance. Many things that are common to all sixteen-year-olds were also common to me but they took on further meaning.

"Take, for instance, the group we spoke of earlier. Group

dates are important to any sixteen-year-old and group relationship is important. But for me, a Negro girl of sixteen, the dates that were available and the places to go were limited. Coupled with the natural conflicts of being alone on a date at sixteen was the added awareness that it was safer when I was with a group. We couldn't go every place we wanted to even if we had the money necessary.

"I was in college in Washington, D.C., when the first-run movie houses were desegregated. The result was that we tore downtown to finally pay our money and sit where we wished. That was an important event to me in college, as important as getting good grades. Occurrences such as these, the symbolic theater being open or not, have affected my life."

Dr. Fuller leaned back and eyed the sheafs of medical reports, write-ups of sessions with patients and applications to a health clinic that were stacked on her dining table. It was 10:30 at night, and her working day had not ended. She stood up, ready to see me to the door.

"Through the years I have been especially fortunate—there were so many teachers who were good to me, interested in me. They always made me feel that they wanted from me the best I had to give, and I in turn felt that they gave me the best they had. I know that not every student has teachers like that. In fact, I think that most of them don't; I've seen more teachers who don't belong in the profession than I can count. But getting that encouragement from an extraordinary group of people has left me with the feeling that I can ask the questions and get the answers which help me to do my job well. There is no more valuable gift they could have given me."

Sybil Christopher

Sybil Christopher, a woman who laughs easily and beautifully, conceived, organized and successfully opened Arthur, the best-known discotheque in New York City.

Sybil was born in Tylorstown, Wales, in 1930. Her mother died when she was ten, and her father when she was fifteen. An older sister, Elsie, looked after the family until Sybil was fourteen. After a year at the London Academy of Music and Dramatic Arts, she heard that Welsh actresses were needed for the film, The Last Days of Dolwyn, *and got a bit part. While making this film, she met Richard Burton—he was playing the lead—and they were married four months later. She was nineteen.*

After her marriage, Sybil Burton devoted herself to rearing their two daughters, Jessica and Kate. In 1964, after fifteen years of marriage, the Burtons were divorced. She decided to move to New York with her daughters, began producing plays and in the spring of 1965 opened Arthur. It was named after a Beatle's reply to the question, "What do you call that haircut?"

In June, 1965, she married Jordan Christopher, leader of The Wild Ones, a rock-and-roll quintet then playing at Arthur. Now the musical director of Arthur, he has also begun a film career and has already appeared in two films: Return of the Seven, *with Yul Brynner, and* The Fat Spy, *with Phyllis Diller.*

Sybil Christopher

New York City's best-known and liveliest discotheque, Arthur, was very quiet at three o'clock in the afternoon. The dance floor was vacant, and deep shadows made it look cavernous, even spooky. But the bar, a smaller room in back, still glowed, and Sybil Christopher's silvery blond hair was one of the first things I saw. As my eyes adjusted, Mrs. Christopher's face materialized. Smiling, she half-rose to shake my hand and then dropped back in her seat, cupping her chin in her hand. She shook her head. "Just look at that carpet," she trilled in a musical Welsh accent. "We put it down only four months ago and already it looks dreadful. Cigarette burns everywhere. It's extraordinary!" (She pronounced it "extrordnry.") "Would you like some tea?"

I had barely nodded yes before she went briskly to the bar to get it. Like her customers, Mrs. Christopher was dressed mod-style: a black-and-white check smock; blunt-cut, straight hair to her shoulders. When she returned with a pot of tea and cups, a waiter was at her heels with sugar and cream.

"It's very strange, you know," she said, "but if people's lives were just written down, fact for fact, on a piece of paper, you could have the most awful misconceptions about them. My early life sounds absolutely tragic. We came from a little industrial town in Wales. My real mother died when I was ten and my father when I was fifteen. Oh, it could break your heart if you didn't know the truth about it. Actually, my childhood was far from tragic.

"The story is rather complicated. I came from the second group of children, because my father's first wife had died. I had two half-sisters, fifteen or twenty years older than I, and they were always looking after the rest of us. My own mother had four babies, three boys and a girl. Perhaps being the only girl from the second group made me confident. I remember thinking at all ages: everyone must want a daughter of thirteen, fourteen, fifteen—whatever age I happened to be at the time. I never doubted that I was cared for.

"I remember being distinctly pleased that I had a certain amount of discipline. My other friends in this little clique I ran around with were like something let loose. I adored them and didn't disapprove of anything they did, but I was glad *I* had restrictions. One night—it was a Saturday night, the big night out in our village—I was sort of goofing around in the back of a café with some of my clique. All of a sudden one of my older sisters appeared and absolutely bellowed: 'Sybil! Get home!' I pretended to object, of course. In fact I acted very angry, and went slouching out in a rage, but all the way home on the bus I was secretly delighted. Naturally. Someone cared about me and what I did. Extraordinary. I think it's because I had this discipline that I nearly always behaved well. Nowadays when I go home to Wales—which I don't do too often—I'm amazed to see my contemporaries, those wild girls who used to act up all the time, looking like middle-aged women.

"I was also lucky because I was extremely close to one of my brothers and he was very helpful. He would actually comment on things, a dress I'd have on, or something of the sort. He'd tell me it was nice and I should wear it more often, things like that. Very unusual for a boy that age to regard his sister as a real human being. I had another brother who was so close to my age that we could never really talk; he was embarrassed by me, I think. Part of it was because I used to date his best friend and he would say to this boy, 'How can you go out with her?' Funny, that. He just couldn't understand it.

"Of course I thought about boys all the time. It was such a tiny village, really minute, and there wasn't much else to do. Going to chapel on Sunday was centered around boys. Everything was, if you were young. For the grownups there was politics.

"The village was called Maerdy" (she made it sound like Mahrdear) "and it was a red-hot communist town. They used to call it Little Moscow. Funny, because there was a village just a few miles away called Ferndale which was just as solidly socialist. The whole valley was socialist as a matter of fact, but Maerdy was a little pocket of absolutely fervent communism. All of my mother's sisters were married to ardent socialists, and on Election Day I used to wear the Labor Rosette. We were considered practically upper class for being socialists. Harry Pollitt, the head of the Communist Party then, was always around talking in our village. Oh, red-hot it was! I remember meeting the English actress Sybil Thorndike many years later, and when I told her I came from Maerdy she said: 'Oh yes, Little Moscow!' Odd I wasn't more politically inclined myself,

[255]

but then none of us were. I was only interested in boys and getting out of school and into the real world.

"I was a dropout, you know. Oh, not that I really hated school, but I wasn't keen on it, and I begged my family for years to let me leave. When my mother died I was ten years old, and my elder half-sister, who was married and living in the Midlands in Northampton, had to come home and look after us. She brought her little daughter Wendy with her, and by the time I was fourteen she had been away from her husband for four years. I kept thinking what a groove it would be for me to stay home all day and look after the family. There was only my father and one brother to take care of—the other brother was in the R.A.F. by this time—and it seemed the most sensible thing to do. So, that's really the way I left school—a matter of necessity. But I was delighted, really delighted. My sister went back to Northampton and I stayed home, simple as that. The only real block was that my father, like every Welsh father, wanted his kids to go into the teaching profession. It took a lot for him to say yes about my dropping out. I guess he could see there was no intellectual future for me. Academically I was a dead loss, very different from my brothers and sisters, who all went to University. But anyway he allowed me to go my own way. Very wise, really. I was of a completely different bent, much more an exhibitionist. None of my brothers or sisters would ever have dreamed of going on the stage, as I later did.

"I think I adjusted very well to my new life. I would get up early in the morning with my father, for all the world like a young married woman, and make breakfast. Everything was always done by 9:30 in the morning. Of course I had the energy of ten mature women. What fun I had in the village shops! When I would go to do my marketing, they would give me all sorts of special attention. I was much younger than everyone else, and I enjoyed it so.

"Of course there were times when everything seemed to go wrong. I might burn something, and my father would come home to find me in tears over it, absolutely heartbroken. I was telling Jordan just the other day about the little notebook I had, like an exercise book. I put all sorts of headings in it like 'How to Cook,' and then underneath I'd make notations like 'Boil potatoes.' Extraordinary. It looked like my chemistry book, but inside were all these notes on how to take care of my family. Once my sister from Northampton visited us, and she told me to mind how much sugar I was using. We were all on ration then, and she told me to save the sugar for Christmas pies and puddings. Well, I took her seriously and by the time Christmas came around there was enough sugar saved—oh, cupboards of it—to bake a hundred Christmas puddings. I had fed everyone with saccharine for months.

"Do you see what I mean?" she said emphatically, putting down her teacup with a click. "If I were just to tell these things bluntly without elaborating you would think, 'Oh, the poor thing, the poor little mite doing all that by herself.' But it wasn't at all that way. I had the most marvelous time.

"I didn't miss school a bit. I thought the teachers had so little imagination. There was no inspiration in hearing them talk. I remember only one, an English teacher, and I can remember quite distinctly that I loved to hear her read poetry. She sort of broke down the barriers, prejudices you form about great literature. You'd be reading, say, Dickens, and she would tell you things that were just unheard-of then. One time she said, 'Suppose you come to a passage that says, "The door opened and there he stood," and you see a lot of description coming up. Well, skip that and go on to the story part. You can always get back to the description later.' Extraordinary. But she was the only one.

"I really do think I learned more staying at home. Having older sisters who were bright gave me a lot of confidence. The teachers used to tell me: 'Oh, you're not nearly as good as your sister Linda.' But it never hurt me. I adored my sisters and was proud of them. We were all so completely different, you see, and when that happens no one is competitive. It's amazing to think they all went on to become teachers themselves, and me a dropout. One of my older brothers teaches art at the University of Cardiff, and the oldest, David, is a perfectly marvelous teacher.

"He has the kind of imagination and spirit my teachers lacked. He taught in an elementary school in Lancashire, and his students were really tough boys. He read them Dylan Thomas and had them loving it. He got each one of those boys to write a novel, and at the end of the term he found a reasonable bookbinder in town and had each of the novels bound up. He had their names put on them, too. You should have seen the looks on those boys' faces when they saw a big, fat book of their own making. I don't know if you can appreciate what an extraordinary accomplishment it was. They were rough kids. He also taught them to play poker in their spare time, and he made up wonderful games for them to play. Sometimes he'd take them out on the street and have them pretend they were reporters for the newspaper. They loved him very much. David rolls his own cigarettes—it would wear you out just to watch him—and at Christmastime they clubbed in and bought him one hundred cigarettes.

"Anyway, the point I'm trying to make is that I was always surrounded by bright, imaginative people who helped greatly to form my opinions, though I myself was an extremely uncurious child. I never even had any great desire to travel. When one of my sisters went to Paris to be an English governess for six months, it seemed as far away as China to me. I have only a vague recollection of being taken to London when I was about eight to see the Coronation. It's all in bits and pieces, sitting on someone's shoulders and seeing the crowds and the flash of diamonds and someone saying, 'That's the Duke of Something-or-Other.' Diamonds and dukes and duchesses—very exciting, of course, but quite remote to me.

"You see, life was very simple then. You went to school and schemed about how to get out and dreamed of what you'd really *like* to do. Usually the dreams were pretty much unformed. I thought I might like to work in a dress shop or be a baby nurse (later I got quite hung up on that idea) or whatever. In the meantime there were boys and family life to fill the time.

"My family life was quite rich and full. I remember particularly Christmases. In a way Christmas should be a tragic time for me, because so many terrible things occurred around then. Both my mother and my little brother died at Christmastime, and yet the family rallied around, and we somehow made something beautiful of those Christmases. We played a lot of paper-and-pencil games and there was a great spirit of closeness. One Christmas my brother gave me a novel. It was the first novel I had ever received which was all my own. Of course I had read the classics in school, but I had never undertaken to read one on my own. I remember very little about the novel itself. What I do remember is the pleasure of receiving a book of my very own.

"I romanticized much more about the movies than I did about books. I was a film-fanatic. I adored Donald O'Connor, and I used to daydream about appearing in a film opposite him—all very obvious stuff. We had only one cinema in Maerdy, of course, and it showed American films. I never missed a Donald O'Connor film, never, and I loved Peggy Ryan and Roddy McDowall. But the marvelous thing was that one didn't have ambitions then. I didn't say to myself, 'Look here, Sybil, what you want to be is a movie star.' I just enjoyed it. Wanting to actually be something came much later. I used to sit in school and long to be somewhere else, but it was never clear where. One day I'd think of working in a shop and the next I'd yearn to be a nursery teacher.

"I even acted in a play then. The chapel Dramatic Society in our village picked me to play Sidney, the girl in *A Bill of Divorcement*. Katharine Hepburn played the part in the film. I just adored the sophistication of it all. The part called for me to smoke, but I was fifteen and I didn't know how. My father taught me and I haven't stopped smoking since. I enjoyed the whole thing just enormously, but the point is I didn't suddenly decide to become an actress after one play in a village drama society. I was happy and secure, and I thought whatever happened would come in good time.

"Everything seemed so uncomplicated then. Take the matter of clothes. Everyone wore uniforms to school, and then on the weekend you had old clothes to knock around in for Saturday and a good dress for Sunday. The clothes and styles were simply ghastly then, but at least we all had pretty much the same to wear and there was no trying to outdo the next girl with fancy dresses and such. I never felt shabby in any way, although I may have been. It just didn't occur to me or anyone else to think that way." Mrs. Christopher threw up her hands: "Maybe I was a very boring teenager, you know? So well-adjusted and confident?

"Anyway, I left Wales just before I was sixteen. My father

died the Christmas of my fifteenth year, and the following March I went to live with my half-sister in Northampton. I had my first job there, in a dress shop, and I immediately joined two societies, a drama club and one called the Northampton Players. They were both amateur, but good. I did about six parts a year with them, some quite wrong for me. Once I played the woman in a play called *They Came to the City* by J. B. Priestley. She was supposed to be twenty-two or twenty-three and I was just sixteen.

"Northampton also had a professional company, and it was repertory, something I'd never seen before. It was really a very good group, what you'd call a number-one company. I remember distinctly sitting in the window of the dress shop where I worked, watching the actors and actresses going by to rehearsals. That's when I began to formulate an actual ambition, which was to become first a juvenile and then a leading lady with a repertory company. Nothing to do with acting in London—that never entered my mind.

"I stayed on in Northampton, but I wanted to go to school in London. It took me a long time to convince my family to let me have a try. I remember my sister saying to me, 'If there's anything else you think you could be happy doing, you should try it.' My family knew I had a great capacity to enjoy most jobs. I enjoyed what I was doing then, too, and the lady in the dress shop took a great interest in me and was very kind, and I was also hung up on the idea of being a nursery teacher. Northampton is a shoe-manufacturing town, and there was a great plan on to hire girls to look after children while their mothers were at work in the factories.

"My family knew I could be happy doing that or any number of other things, and they wondered 'Why theater?' In the meantime I had auditioned for the Northampton Repertory, but they had tremendously high standards and I knew I would have to go to a proper school if I ever wanted to act with a good rep company. I don't know if you can imagine what it was like for me in Northampton. I don't know what the equivalent would be here in America—to come from the depths of Wales with a really strong Welsh accent and find myself meeting the sort of people I met. Many of the actors in the amateur group had worked with professionals during the war. Mad keen, they were, and the people I met at the dress shop, so completely different from my friends back home in Wales. It was such an exciting time for me. I was very happy. At first I wrote to my girlfriends back home constantly, at least once a week, and then it gradually dropped off. I think you always have to get away from home in a way. Everything was so new.

"Of course now kids are discovering things for themselves much earlier. When I compare myself at that age to the kids I see today, I feel that I had my head in the sand. They seem so much more aware and brighter. I'm not sure what's caused it—a lot of things, I'm sure, all coming together. People like the Beatles suddenly arriving. At first they were kind of a joke, and then suddenly they became something to reckon with.

"There's so much to become involved with now. In England I think immediately of the Beatles and the Royal Ballet and people queuing up to see them. It's important to be young today. Young people make up an incredibly large percentage of our population. Of course the cinema-going and record-buying public is overwhelmingly youthful. For perhaps the first time we must please the teenagers, which I think is marvelous. They have caused us to pour millions of dollars into art. They're important and they know it.

"They have a look now, too. When I was young, there was no

look—clothes, hair, styles. Everything was ghastly. I think it's wonderful that someone like Mary Quant exists. We had absolutely nobody like her when I was young. The styles are so great, they've got so much going for them. And Streisand— what she's done for teenagers! She's made certain concepts of beauty obsolete. The traditional dolly-face seems a little silly now. One wants to have a face and a profile, a look that represents character. Think of someone like Edith Sitwell; how marvelous she would have been as a teenager today. I don't know if you read her book, but she suffered such pain over being plain and eccentric. There would have been no need for that today at all.

"The kids who come in here, you know straightaway who they're hung up on by how they look, and yet they're individuals too. Wonderful!"

I mentioned a short story I had read about teenagers taking over the world, putting up idols of rock 'n roll singers, passing laws to lower the voting age to fourteen and establishing retirement camps for people over thirty-five. Mrs. Christopher said it sounded like the work of a brilliant writer named Robert Thom, and so it was.

"He's doing a screenplay now," she said. "He has an incredible imagination. Frightening. But the point is that young people will be heard. They're insisting on it, and they're a majority and they deserve consideration.

"Time was when no one listened to their needs or demands. I happened to be very lucky in that someone always seemed to be taking an interest in me. For example, the lady who owned the dress shop in Northampton wanted to send me to London to train as a window-dresser. It was a nice idea, but by that time I was pretty set on theater.

"I used to practice on the job. When new customers came in

I would wait on them using different accents, things like that. And meanwhile I was watching the rep company people pass the shop on their way to rehearsal and thinking about how I could get to school in London. It took me a long time to convince my family, but when they finally gave in they were wonderful. We decided I should audition for the Royal Academy of Dramatic Art, so off I went to London. I was trying for a very important scholarship called the Leverhume, and I was in competition with a lot of others. I think six hundred auditioned that year. I had heard they were very careful to disenchant anyone who didn't come up to their standards, and after you auditioned you had to wait for some time while they decided. Well, I went home to Northampton and three weeks later a very bright sort of letter arrived telling me I didn't quite have what it took to be accepted by R.A.D.A. and I'd probably be happier doing something else. Of course I just burst into tears, utterly desolate.

"But I had a little money my father had left me, so I made plans to enroll in a drama school called L.A.M.D.A. in London. It was supposed to be an excellent school, but I had had my heart set on the Royal Academy.

"Here I was, getting ready to go to London, and on Christmas Eve a letter arrived from R.A.D.A. telling me there had been a mix-up. I'd received the wrong letter, and what do you know? I'd placed fourth out of the six hundred who auditioned! Honestly, it was like a happy ending in the movies. Extraordinary. I hadn't won the Leverhume Scholarship, but they offered me a greatly reduced fee. But I'd already enrolled in the other school, so the letter arrived too late.

"I went to London, and like all good Welsh girls I stayed with an auntie. L.A.M.D.A. turned out to be marvelous. It was a very 'with-it' school, and more men and boys went there than to R.A.D.A. I received great training there. First of all, you spent twenty-four hours a day thinking about yourself, for better or worse. And you learned *everything,* costumes and makeup and lighting as well as dramatic training. There's nothing like it in America. After each term L.A.M.D.A. put on a show, and every agent in London was there. People were picked straight from school to go on to the West End and films. It's all so much easier in England. The film studios are right there in London and there's no traveling three thousand miles to Hollywood. It's all centralized, and if you have good training there's no difficulty in getting work. American actors have a much harder time of it. There's no repertory system to train them and sometimes I wonder how they ever do it. You have to have a great ambition, I guess.

"I was very unambitious, really. Rachel Roberts, who is a marvelous actress, used to laugh with me about our lack of ambition. It all seemed such great fun. Rachel used to say, 'When you're with someone who's *really* dedicated, you can always tell. There's nothing quite like it.' Of course she went on to become a truly magnificent actress. There's no one quite like her. I wonder if maybe she didn't have more ambition than she realized.

"I adored everything about theater, the dressing rooms, makeup, costumes—everything about it except actually going onstage. That part made me rather miserable. Very nervous I was. I went immediately from school to a play in the West End, an American play, *Harvey,* the one about the eight-foot invisible rabbit. I did a film on my holiday and then went to Stratford on Avon. You see, there was no end to the amount one could work.

"Rachel was at Stratford, too, and neither of us ever thought we'd get anything but a walk-on. Then I landed the role of the

Welsh princess in *Henry IV*, a dream part, and Rachel played Ceres, one of the goddesses in *The Tempest*. We weren't really very jubilant or excited, because we felt much of our freedom had gone. We didn't have as much time to knock about, and we'd get together and complain. I began to think about how I didn't really enjoy being on the stage. I was a real theater lover all right, but the acting itself made me terribly nervous. I suppose everyone's nervous onstage, but I didn't even seem to find much fulfillment in it. I loved the life but disliked the acting. I think that's partly to do with my not really being ambitious.

"One good thing, Rachel and I were both encouraged to keep our Welsh accents. They told us there were plenty of girls around with standard English accents and we should hang on to what was obviously so much a part of us. I was very lucky—everything I ever succeeded in onstage was done with a Welsh accent.

"Actually, the funny thing is I never really could speak Welsh. I can read it and understand it, and I know enough to say a few words to another Welsh person, but the grammar is appalling. I think I left home at a very good time. Going to London when I did saved me from becoming a professional Welshman. London is full of them, and nothing is more tedious. I'm terribly proud of being Welsh, but there's always the danger of confusing pride with coyness. When I was a little girl, I was sure the Bible was translated from Welsh into English, because all the chapel services were in Welsh. One thing—there were colored people and Jewish people and Indians in our village, and one never thought of them as anything but Welsh. Absolutely no problems of discrimination there. Oh, maybe in the big industrial towns, but in the little villages, never. The only time you ever referred to a person as anything

other than Welsh was if you were lucky enough to be signed
up with an Indian doctor under National Health. The Indian
doctors were greatly looked up to, almost a mystical thing, and
people would say: 'Oh, he's brilliant. He's an *Indian.*'

"I will always stress the fact I'm Welsh rather than English.
My part of Wales, the south, is so ugly it's marvelous. The
northern part is staggeringly beautiful, as lovely as any place in
the world. Still, all the talent comes out of the south: Dylan
Thomas and the great painters."

A young man in a trenchcoat came in just then, and her face
lit up. "Hello, peach," she said and introduced her husband,
Jordan Christopher. Briefly they discussed a group which had
auditioned for Arthur. "Gimmicky," said Mrs. Christopher,
wrinkling her nose. Jordan agreed. They decided to have dinner at Arthur that night and then with a smile directed to Sybil
and a " 'Bye, darling," he was off.

"We love it here," she said. "Love Arthur. All the kids who
come are so marvelous. My daughter Kate is only nine, but her
heroine is Jean Shrimpton. How great kids are today. I was so
naive by comparison. I think if I had to tell my kids any one
thing it would be: 'Don't care too much about what other
people think of you.' If Kate has a new dress and some of her
friends say it's too short, I tell her to explain nicely that that's
the way they wear them in Europe. Kate is very American, but
she's Welsh too. She'd like to go to University at Oxford, which
delights me.

"Then there's the business of restrictions being placed on
children. I know that Kate appreciates having certain regulations to follow, just as I did. I've been so lucky, really. My
family always handled me exactly right. About theater, for
example. They tried to discourage me, but when they saw I
was determined they gave me all the confidence and encour-

agement in the world. I found out for myself that acting wasn't really for me.

"I never intended to marry early. In fact, I remember at sixteen I decided I wouldn't marry until late in life, about twenty-seven. Loads of my pals rushed to get married, and it seemed to me a mad thing to tie yourself down so young. And then, of course, I got married at nineteen. So you never know. From then on acting assumed a very secondary part in my life. After all, the most important thing in theater is getting up in front of an audience. In the end that's all that matters, and I never enjoyed that anyway. Once I became a wife the rest began to fade away. But I needed that chance to prove myself. I think it's terribly important to get away from home at some point.

"I like to think of my family as a rock. We hardly ever write, yet when there's the need, as there was last year when something ghastly happened to one of my brother's children, we're all together solidly like a rock. It sometimes seems extraordinary to me even now to be an adult, a grownup. Yet I am, and I don't need my family any more. I know they're there and I can always depend on them, which is as it should be."

We had drunk all the tea. Mrs. Christopher had another appointment. She turned her palms up and said, "That's really all I have to say about myself. I hope I wasn't so well-adjusted when I was young that reading about me will be a bore." She called goodbye and left me to Arthur's late-afternoon half-light. A few hours later, scores of people would be queuing up, as she would say, for a night of music and dancing.

Jacquelyn Anderson Mattfeld

Jacquelyn Anderson's parents were university students when she was born in Baltimore, Maryland, in 1925; she has been in or around schools ever since. As a girl she studied music and was already teaching piano in her late high school years. A scholarship in piano took her to the Peabody Conservatory in Baltimore, where she studied for three years. In 1948, she took her bachelor's degree in music from Goucher College (she was elected to Phi Beta Kappa), but decided against a career as a professional musician.

She continued her studies in music history at the Graduate School of Yale University and she married a classmate, Victor Henry Mattfeld (now editor-in-chief of the Schirmer Music Company). Her first child, Stefanie, was born in 1953, and a second daughter, Felicity, in 1954. During this period she combined motherhood and scholarship, working as a research assistant in the Yale University Department of Music History. She received her doctorate from Yale in 1959.

Since then, she has held various administrative jobs in a number of universities. In 1959, she came to Radcliffe College, first as Director of Financial Aid and then as Associate Dean of Student Affairs and Dean of East House. Simultaneously, she was busy teaching and writing. She lectured in music history at Harvard Graduate School and found time to write an occasional article, book review and review of program notes. In 1963 she was invited to become Associate Dean of Student Affairs at the Massachusetts Institute of Technology; as such, she assumed primary reponsibility for graduate and undergraduate women students at the Institute.

In 1965, Mrs. Mattfeld was appointed Dean of Sarah Lawrence College in Bronxville, New York. She came to this post, she says, in a spirit of adventure. Her double interests in musical scholarship and college administration are reflected in the writing she has done since 1961. She has written, for example, on both the Renaissance composer Josquin des Prés and on the role of the educated woman in our society. But her deepest commitment is to "the human purposes of liberal education" and, what follows naturally from that, to helping Sarah Lawrence affirm and achieve those purposes for its teachers and students.

Jacquelyn Anderson Mattfeld

DEAN MATTFELD shook my hand from behind her large desk. Framed in back of her, through a bank of windows, was a traditional campus view—green lawns flanked on one side by mellow brick pseudo-Tudor buildings and on the other by dormitories recently designed by architect Philip Johnson. The contrast is telling. Sarah Lawrence was, in fact, only founded in 1928.

The dean's office itself is entirely contemporary and skillfully decorated in contrasting colors—grapes and greens, blues against white. There is a sculpture that might be by Jean Arp and an abstract painting in the style of Jackson Pollock.

Dean Mattfeld is tall and very slender. She speaks in a soft contained voice. Her gestures are small but definite, her wavy blond hair wispy and casual in style. She smiles rarely, but a smile can catch her face unawares and illuminate it. She wore a vivid blue wool shift, and when I commented that she and the room seemed to match, she said, "It's a happy accident. The colors of the Osver painting over there are my colors, so when we redecorated the office last summer, it seemed sensible to plan the color scheme around the painting.

"You know," she began, "what seems odd to me is that so many married women who don't work believe that a woman with a job, or especially a *profession,* is somehow not living up to her responsibilities as a woman—just because she doesn't also do all her own housework or work for the PTA. Nobody questions the masculinity of a professional man who doesn't repair his car, shovel the snow or put out the garbage. But there seem to be a good many people who assume that the professional woman who doesn't scrub her floors, do all the cooking and mending, and chauffeur the children is not really feminine. Many of us who have both families and professions do attend to a lot of the details of the housekeeping side of homemaking, but that doesn't prove anything about whether or not we make happy and loving wives and mothers.

"To judge by most of the short stories and feature articles in women's magazines, there must be a lot of people who are still equating being a real woman and being a good wife and mother with being in the house all day, whether or not anyone else is there, and with doing housework to the exclusion of everything else. It's a real anomaly, don't you think? I mean educating men *and* women will hopefully lead to a society in which people are largely freed from routine labor, so that they will have more time and insights and skills to use in relationships and creative activities which make life better and more satisfying for themselves and others.

"I guess one reason I am so totally happy at Sarah Lawrence is that it is my kind of community and these are my kind of people. More than half of the faculty are men, but they are men who take it for granted that women are people and are worth educating. Most of the faculty (and some of the students, too) agree it's just a matter of time until we become coeducational, but they still think educating women is a serious and important concern. They enjoy teaching young women and appreciate the special interests and thought processes that make working with them different than teaching men. I think this feeling creates a tone in the Sarah Lawrence classroom that frees women to be themselves: there is less pretense and self-consciousness among Sarah Lawrence students than among women students in other schools I've known. And that's not just my opinion—the visitors who come to the college always comment on the open manner and wonderful articulateness of Sarah Lawrence girls. It's a special place, I think.

"This is the fifth major institution I've been a part of, in one capacity or another, and I've loved them all; but if someone were to give me eighty million dollars or so, and say 'design a college,' I'd come up with something very like Sarah Lawrence. I like the emphasis on the individual, on being open to new ideas and new ways of doing things, and on people talking to people. I believe one hundred percent in the importance of having people of different generations talk about matters of real concern to them, and that's what happens in a small class of twelve or fifteen students. Reading and discussion aren't the only ways of teaching and learning, of course, but I think they remain one of the most satisfying to students and rewarding for the faculty. At Sarah Lawrence we put a lot of emphasis on independent study and on field work, but the real backbone of our instruction is small discussion classes and individual tutorials.

"Our system isn't perfect, and we're like all the other colleges today—always in a state of self-examination and always trying to find better ways of helping students work out their educational problems and find themselves. But the great thing is that almost all of us here are people-centered, so we find this kind of informal and flexible college made to order. The result is, we're congenial and respect each other's opinions, which makes for a healthy situation for the students *and* the teachers.

"You know, I didn't just discover Sarah Lawrence when I was asked to be dean. I really found out about it when I was a senior in high school. I was sixteen and trying to decide where I could go to college and what I wanted to do with my life. I stumbled on a Sarah Lawrence catalogue in the high school library and became a devotée on the spot. In 1942 Sarah Lawrence was really considered 'way out' with its ideas about no grades and no required courses. But what really appealed to me right then was that they gave credit for music—at that time in my life I was pulled between wanting to be a doctor, loving art and literature, and wanting to be a pianist. I also had a long-standing dream of going away to Bryn Mawr College, I guess because my mother had had her freshman year there and regaled me with wonderful tales of her experiences. But as it turned out, there really wasn't any chance of my going to Sarah Lawrence or Bryn Mawr. Even if I'd had a scholarship, it just wouldn't have been possible for my parents to scrape up the additional money to send me away. I went to Goucher because I could live at home and commute, and because they gave me a very big scholarship. But at the time it was a big disappointment."

I asked Dean Mattfeld about her parents, and she paused a moment, in the manner of someone used to reflecting over questions, before she answered. "My parents are absolutely different from each other in temperament. When I was in my teens, I remember wondering how on earth they had ever decided to get married when they so clearly hadn't a thing in common as people. Their backgrounds were altogether different, too. My father is of Scotch-Irish parentage—he and his brother were the first of the family to finish high school, let alone college. Both of them worked their way through Penn State—washing dishes, scrubbing floors and cleaning stables. My uncle majored in engineering and my father majored in agricultural chemistry. When I think back on it, I realize that he was one of those rare people who come up the hard way but never tell their children how much easier life is for them than it was for their parents.

"My grandparents on that side were working-class people who had come to the United States in one of the waves of immigration that followed an Irish potato famine. My grandfather was a big, burly man—loud, demonstrative and generous to a fault. He could never refuse a friend who asked for a loan, and he couldn't manage money. At different times in his life he owned a greenhouse, a coal business and a small dairy. But he lost them all and eventually became a milkman. When he retired at sixty-five he was miserable without people to talk to, and so he leased a small gas station where he worked until he was eighty-five. Everybody knew and liked him for miles around, and children came in and out of the station all day long to talk to him and get him to fix things.

"His wife, my grandmother Anderson, was quite different. She was an avid reader and made biweekly pilgrimages to the town library where she literally read every book, fiction and nonfiction, on the subject of American history. She was a stickler for doing things right, and I remember my distress when I could never set the table or make a bed or sew a seam in her house without constant corrections from her. But she was really a very fine person, and as I got into my teens I began to discover that she was fun to talk to about *her* growing-up years and even about American history, which in those days I didn't really think was very interesting at all. I remember her counting out a coffee jar full of small change every Saturday night and writing figures in a neat round hand in ledgers. But it was years before I realized that she had kept all the books for my grandfather's various enterprises, and had managed to save up enough in nickels and dimes to keep them completely independent financially until they died in their late eighties.

"My mother's parents were quite different. They were second cousins, impoverished post-Civil War gentility from Tennessee, and they were terribly proud of their background. I remember puzzling over why they seemed to feel superior to Northerners. They kept very careful track of their family trees and felt strong family loyalty to 'kin,' even distantly related. When I was little I was embarrassed by all of the kissing and hugging and exclaiming that went on at the huge family gatherings they held a couple of times a year, but as I got into my teens I became interested in knowing about the personalities and lives of the people who had come before me on both sides of my family. Then I loved to get them to talk and show me old family pictures and letters.

"My grandmother was a tall and willowy lady, nearly five foot ten and very beautiful. She was injured in a bicycle accident as a girl and was lame all her life from a badly-set, broken hip. She was a painter—not completely an amateur, either, since she supported herself for some years—until she married at thirty—by selling her water colors and painted china. Come to think of it, I guess I come from a long line of working women, because *her* mother had run a dame school [a school held in the teacher's home] and had tutored young men preparing for college in Greek and Latin.

"Anyway, I used to pump my grandmother for accounts of

her life, and gradually both she and my grandfather became important friends of mine. They were both tremendously anxious for me to finish my schooling, and wrote me regularly— long, loving, supporting letters—all the time I was in high school, college, conservatory and graduate school. They believed in me and told me again and again in all those letters how much they loved me and were proud of me and what great things they expected of me. Nowadays people get embarrassed by that sort of Victorian floweriness, but I think there's a lot to be said for letting people you care about know it.

"Both of them were really anxious for me to go to college— partly, I know, because they had wanted to and had never been able to. My grandfather had to drop out of school and go to work after the third grade when his father died. He had a near genius for selling things, and was absolutely indefatigable. Somehow he managed to earn enough to support his mother and sister and to send his brother to law school. All his life he was financing somebody's way through college—distant cousins, and sometimes young people he just met on his travels as a hardware drummer and thought needed a break. Both he and my grandmother believed that no matter what you had, you shared it. But it was my grandfather who had the most remarkable faith in human nature and in the importance of education. It was a terrible disappointment to him that he had no sons and that neither of his two daughters finished college.

"My mother went to the Baldwin School and then to Bryn Mawr. She met my father on a blind date when she was fifteen, and at the end of her freshman year they got married. Both their families thoroughly disapproved, but they were very much in love and decided they had waited long enough. They went off to Baltimore and set up housekeeping on twenty-five dollars a week. I was born in Baltimore. My sister was born two years later, but she died when she was four. All my earliest memories are of student life. We lived in a third-floor apartment of a typical Baltimore row house. My father was going to night school at Johns Hopkins University and working on his Ph.D., and my mother had entered Goucher to go on with her undergraduate studies. The apartment was halfway between the two schools, and it was full of students, days, nights and weekends. There were all sorts of romances and intellectual discussions going on around us, and I remember the sense of security and happiness we had. Sometimes Mother took us to classes with her—we were pretty good at playing blocks under the desks. We were used as guinea pigs for the girls who were psychology and education majors, and we took more IQ tests than most people do in a lifetime. We loved the ceremonies that went on, too—daisy chains and step-singing by lantern light and academic processions with all the bright colors and fancy robes.

"They were good years. I think probably one reason that I really enjoy the 'full house' that goes with deaning is that I have always had such happy memories of that period of my life. It has always seemed important and natural to open one's home to friends. In fact, my parents never made the distinction between friends and family that so many people do. No matter who dropped in at mealtime, there was always enough to go around, and no matter how many people dropped in or at what hour, my mother and father were really glad to see them and made them feel at home. Somehow they got across to us children that it wasn't blood ties or religious ties or backgrounds that were important, but the pleasure people got from each other's company when they really liked one another. It seems to me that there was always conversation and laughter in the house, and I grew up knowing it was important to work hard, but just as important to be ready to stop and talk and listen whenever people were around to share with.

"Even when I was in my middle teens and worried a lot about not belonging to any community or social group, I admired my parents' way of making anybody I brought home feel at ease and accepted into the family. I found it pretty hard to bring new friends home, though. I was self-conscious about my mother's broad *a,* and the fact that the house was so shabby and my mother never did any cleaning because she hated housework. And it bothered me then that we seemed not to fit into any kind of category—other people who were poor like us spoke a different kind of English and didn't have a *Webster's Unabridged Dictionary* or the *Encyclopaedia Britannica.* People who read as much as we did and were as passionately interested in ideas as we were didn't eat in the kitchen and have orange crates for bedside tables.

"In high school I began to feel more self-assured, and my senior year—the year I was sixteen—was really a happy one. Not that I didn't have my share of difficulties. I felt miserably awkward in my hand-me-down clothes, and some of the girls I wanted desperately to be accepted by, teased me about my big words and said I was burning the midnight oil to get grades. I had a mad crush on a handsome young teacher who was my first man-teacher, and at the same time I was worrying about how to handle the boy I was going steady with when he said he thought we should plan to get married in five years.

"But lots else was going on, too. I played varsity fieldball and basketball, and belonged to a senior girl scout troop that did pioneer camping, and I was on the debating team. That year, I taught Sunday school and sang in a church choir and accompanied the high school glee club on the piano, too. Playing the piano had become an awfully important part of my life by then. I had waited for years for music lessons, but it wasn't until my sophomore year of high school that my parents found a way to get a used piano and arrange with a teacher for lessons. My piano teacher was a wonderful older friend to me, and I admired her tremendously. She understood, I think, just how good it was for me to have the piano as an outlet for all the intense feelings that go with being an adolescent. I wrote a lot too—poetry and essays—but playing seemed to me the quintessence of sharing deep feelings. That year I played my first full-length solo piano recital. It was a big moment in my life.

"Then, that winter, war was declared and that changed so much in our lives. I remember how bitter and critical we were of our parents' generation which had fought the First World War to end wars, and then had somehow gotten us all into another mess worse than the first. We had two really fine teachers that year—one in English and one in American history—and they let us talk and talk about how we felt and what we thought should have been done to prevent the war. I was in a class of forty boys and girls who were fast learners, and as teachers were drafted and left to work in factories, a couple of us were used instead of substitute teachers. It was wonderful experience, and while we complained about how we were not being well prepared for college—and we weren't—we were secretly proud of having been chosen to teach those classes. I think students now are a lot better informed than we were about political and social affairs of the day. But their *feelings* about war and injustice and the need for strong ethical leadership in education and government are very like those we had way back, twenty-five years ago.

"The year after I graduated from high school, I taught music in an interracial fellowship house in a slum area in Baltimore— just because I wanted to. It was not the popular thing to do then, as it is now, and I lost a lot of my private piano students because of it. My mother was wonderful in backing me up on this project. We didn't get along at all at that point in my life, but even then there were areas of conviction and interest we shared so completely that the painful years of mother-daughter conflict couldn't destroy them.

"I think all adolescents have to go through a lot of turmoil to separate themselves clearly enough from their families to be sure of who they are. But it's just as painful for each one. Knowing it's a normal part of growing up doesn't help while you're going through it, that's for sure. At least that was true for me. My mother is a strong personality—brilliant, hot-tempered and pretty unpredictable. She had worked all through the worst of the Depression while I was in grade school, and I had had a lot of independence. I used to spend most of my after-school hours and most Saturdays wandering in the Baltimore Museum of Art, the Museum of Natural History and the Enoch Pratt Library. I got around the city by myself, fixed meals and picked out my own clothes—all by the time I was eight. My parents talked to me like an adult and expected a lot of me.

"Then suddenly, when I was in the eighth grade, my brother was born and everything changed. I had romanticized what it would be like to have my mother home all the time, and I wasn't expecting things to be difficult. But they were. Mother was not used to being at home, and suburbia was not for her. She felt tied down by a house and a new baby—much as she wanted both—and looking back on it, I know she was lonely and unhappy. Meanwhile I was becoming an adolescent, and I had lots of mixed feelings about that baby brother, even if they were under the surface. I wasn't used to having Mother around to question me about my comings and goings, and I resented her reading my mail and listening in on my phone calls.

"My father stayed out of our battles, but I even minded that because I felt he ought to say who he thought was right. He managed to retreat behind a book or into his lab in the cellar when things got really hot, but most of the time he looked quietly detached and slightly amused, which I think exasperated my mother as much as it did me.

"I left home at seventeen, and it really wasn't until after I was married and had my first baby that my mother and I began to be congenial again. I have a deep regard for the values my parents have given me and no amount of clashes of personality could ever change that. As I've grown older, I've also come to admire the special kind of courage they've had in living the way they wanted to live—according to what they thought was important, regardless of what other people did or thought. I just hope I can live a life as free of sham and pretext.

"I've gotten so much from my parents. My father set high standards and gave me lots of practice in learning to make decisions, even hard ones. I think I got my self-control from him, too. It's hard for me to lose my temper or let off steam, and that's not altogether good, but it is useful sometimes in the kind of work I do. I think I get my great gusto for living from my mother. People are my greatest delight and my reason for being. I've had as many problems and struggles as anybody else, but I've been especially fortunate in having had remarkable and lasting friendships, and a profession that is wonderfully satisfying because it puts all of my interests and all of my life experience to some positive use for other people. Everything gets used for somebody else's good all the time.

"Because I enjoy my home and my husband and daughters just as much as my profession, I go on feeling the tug between the two aspects of my life. But I wouldn't have it different. I know that having a mother who is a college dean is not easy for our daughters. They're bound to have some difficulties because of my personality and the life I've chosen to lead, but they would have had other problems if I had been another person or chosen a different life pattern. Nobody grows up without some struggle—the butterfly has to make his own way out of the chrysalis or he can never fly.

"I think it's still hard for girls growing up in our country to make a real commitment to much of anything. We just don't encourage girls to believe that it's important for them to give themselves wholeheartedly to an interest or pursuit, because we imply, or tell them explicitly, that getting into college and getting married are their only real goals. Higher education and marriage are very, very important, but neither excludes the other and both require that you go on growing. Freud said that love and work are the two great wellsprings of life. To experience the great satisfactions of either, women have to be willing to be clearly defined people."

The phone rang and Dean Mattfeld picked it up. Her expression became intent as she spoke and listened. When she hung up, she said, "I'm afraid I have to keep another appointment. But let me say this final thing. Students often tell me that they don't see how they can squeeze into one lifetime all they want to do and be. I always answer with what I've learned from my own life so far: you can probably have most of what you want—if you're willing to work hard and to accept the fact that you can't have everything all at once."

I left her smiling at her desk, framed against the view of the college, exactly where she wanted to be.

Brenda Ueland

Brenda Ueland has always had a healthy regard for the rightness of her own feelings and ideals. Born in 1892, she grew up in a square white wooden house built by her father on the south shore of Lake Calhoun in Minneapolis, Minnesota. She loved the lake, horses and walking, and her girlhood ideal was a chivalrous knight.

A rigorous life was characteristic of her family. Her father had emigrated to America and become a laborer to put himself through law school. Besides Brenda there were seven sisters and brothers with strong-sounding Viking names like Sigurd, Arnulf, Rolf and Torvald.

Brenda was chunky as a girl, and in high school this was a cause of embarrassment: "I had very strong and serious feelings, I know, but I covered them with jokes." In 1909 she entered Wells College in Aurora, New York. There, to her surprise, her classmates thought her "a card." "They would remark, 'Say, Ueland is fresh,' and a delightful feeling came into me."

After three years at Wells she thirsted for "real life" and transferred to Barnard College in New York City. A few years after graduation she returned to Greenwich Village, barely subsisting on a small allowance from her father and on free-lance writing assignments, such as a double-page spread on "Famous Bachelors" for Every Week, *a magazine that sold for three cents a copy. In Greenwich Village, and later, she had "scores of remarkable non-eminent friends, and there were eminent ones, too, including Carl Sandburg, Robert Penn Warren, Dimitri Mitropoulos, Strangler Lewis and others."*

She married in 1916 and had a daughter, Gabriel—"my witty and intelligent companion." But she found this marriage, as her two later ones, incompatible with her ideal of "true friendship. There was a sunshiny divorce, a chivalrous handshake," and then she took a regular job as a writer for a magazine in Newark, New Jersey. She went on to free-lance for The Ladies' Home Journal, The Saturday Evening Post *and other magazines.*

In 1929, she and her daughter returned to Minneapolis, where she continued to write columns and articles, "not making any money to speak of." Her autobiography, called simply Me, *was published in 1938, and recently she has written a biography of her mother,* Clara Hampson of Minnesota.

When the war in Europe was won in 1945, the Minneapolis Times, *for which she had been writing a daily column, sent her to Norway as a correspondent. There she covered the Quisling trial and had a special mission as well: to locate surviving Norwegian relatives of Minnesotans. The* Times *announced her mission and in two days got fifteen hundred replies. For her work, she received the St. Olav Medal from Norway's King Haakon VII.*

Brenda Ueland

B RENDA UELAND came hurrying into the living room of her daughter's New York apartment. At seventy-five, she leaned forward with energy and bounce, not age. "Hello, hello," she said, beaming. She wore a tailored mulberry suit, and at the collar was a pretty Paisley scarf tied in a bow. She radiated cheerfulness and good health and often there was humor just below the surface of what she said. Indeed, "jokey" is a favorite word of hers.

Physically, the word she suggests is robust, and yet her outward bearing can vary remarkably from minute to minute. Her voice changes often, from high-pitched and quick to a more measured pace. When she was excited or determined about a subject, I noticed her strong, slightly curved nose. Other times, as when she listened, her hands were folded in her lap and she seemed small and owl-like, perched on the couch solely to take in what I was saying. Always, her gaze was direct, measuring but receptive.

"At sixteen, I was in Minneapolis, Minnesota. It was 1907, the most wonderful time the world has ever seen, probably: no war, beautiful country, not cars but horses and carriages, a pony, a cow, a green lake, tennis, beautiful red-cheeked, pretty people around; nobody cross, nobody drunk. Wonderful time in Minneapolis.

"We lived in the country, we thought far in the country, four miles from the courthouse. You had to get there by carriage. It was kind of a big house—two Scandinavian maids, a hired man and freedom. I was in high school. My mother was passionately public spirited and a great democrat, and she believed in public schools. Public schools in those times were awfully nice because in those days, as I say, everybody was nice.

"I wish we all lived back there now. No, I'm not disillusioned—well, yes, perhaps a little bit disillusioned. I think we're under sad pressures today, aesthetically and every way. The haste and the cacophony, the uproar today—the pressures are bad. This sounds so mournful, but I'm not mournful at all. But the kind of Chekhovian silences at night then! Insects, frogs—you could hear for three miles, you could hear oarlocks on the lake. With combustion engines, you can't hear a thing. There's a great roar now which everybody is used to. If you're walking, you're nervous because you're not going thirty miles an hour. But in those days, there was far more poetry, I think, natural poetry of people. My childhood was just extraordinarily Arcadian because of such darling parents.

"Now about me being sixteen: I'll tell you my agonies. No, they weren't agonies. They were good-natured and cheerful times, but I felt I was too fat, and I think I was. I've been told since it wasn't as awful as I think. I was athletic and jovial and very well. I had great freedom, had no sense of anguish or sorrow that I know of.

"But my mother made one kind of sad mistake about me just then. We were country children, you know—we had our mittens on strings till we were about seventeen. Then she thought, 'It's time for Brenda to go to meet some of my city friends, some of these much more stylish, downtown people.' So she had me go to a dancing school, and there I was a wallflower. I was the girl for whom they had the Paul Jones. You go around in two circles hand over hand until the dancing teacher blows her whistle, seeing poor Brenda. The boys didn't ask her to dance. When you get to the boy, she blows her whistle, and he's supposed to dance with you, but he feigns confusion and dances with the girl behind. Well, I hadn't any interest in boys especially, so that my attitude became scornful, jovial-scornful, toward seventeen-year-old boys, suitors. I had brothers and, heavens, I could play football myself.

"But I think that episode affected my life in this way: when I was fairly young, I never had the experience of rejection, jilting, jealousy. At sixteen, you're supposed to learn the agonies of love, in homeopathic doses, but I didn't learn. My great success was later, at twenty-two, in New York City. I was the queen of Greenwich Village, you might say, one of the best running queens they ever had.

"But, as I say, in our family we didn't develop quickly. Mother thought it was all right to stay sort of young and bouncy and lazy. There would be plenty of time to be grown-up. She thought we shouldn't get old and cross before our time. There's something in that, too.

"There were boys around. They liked me, but I was jeering and contemptuous. I didn't mind them as friends, but that ishy stuff—how terrible! My mother said, very gently, 'Brenda, I think you should be a little more encouraging to Harold. He's nice. Why don't you?' That filled me with such indignation—

my own mother asking me to flirt—that I remember going down to our lake (we lived on a lake) and for the first time smoking cigarettes. I smoked cigarettes in revenge for the parental outrage, for being asked to be coy, to be arch.

"Cigarettes meant freedom to me, too. We were coming into suffrage then, and there was still the double standard for men and women. Our family didn't like that—my mother was a great feminist. I remember an old friend used to come out to see us at the lake. One time she said all the Ueland children were boys. The next time she came out she said they were all girls. It was because we would dress, you know, either way. My mother had a theory that the boys could have long hair to their shoulders, and the girls short hair, if they felt like it. She believed in work, but the boys didn't wait on the girls, and the girls weren't menials to the boys. In our family, the boys made beds too. Of course, we girls did the same, but we could also chop wood. Any work was fine. And we could walk twenty miles alone. Mother never scared us by saying, 'Look out for the awful men!' So we were very brave, and the boys were, too.

"I can remember feelings of love at sixteen. For instance, my sister, Anne, had the most adorable young man in love with her. Love, there was plenty of love. But it was going to a band concert or for a drive in the country, and talking and laughing and joking. Kissing was kind of shocking—unattractive, unaesthetic—there was a little overtone of that. Then, on Sundays —this was about 1907, and of course automobiles began to appear later—we'd drive downtown in our carriage, around beautiful shining Lake Calhoun. Here's the boulevard going around, and all the chivalry and beauty of Minneapolis would come driving out: Mrs. Lowry bowing in her victoria, and dashing young men in their phaetons. We'd drive over to the band concert at the lake just beyond us, and downtown was full of horses and wagons. Even now I could hitch up a horse at twenty below zero in the barn—and in the dark. I could do that now.

"Every house in the country had a barn in the back yard, a darling barn with the little cupola, and hay and oats and a horse and a carriage in that barn. You didn't have to be wealthy at all to have that. I remember a kind of Mrs. Back-stitch joke. We had a horse and a neighbor of ours was so indignant when the tax assessor assessed her horse, Nelly, less than our horse, Bessie. Oh, we often went horseback riding, and the mornings were so wonderful. You'd wake up at four, and you'd hear the distant clopping of hooves. Dirt roads, no cars on the roads, and coming around the lake there would be the milk wagons and hay wagons.

"I went East to Wells College after I had finished high school in Minneapolis. A beautiful bucolic college, I might tell you—red cheeks again. All the girls had photographs of their fiancés, and I had no fiancé to my joy and thought, 'Well!' I went there for three years. Then I had an older sister in New York working in a settlement house, and I wanted to watch that: I wanted to see the socialists and anarchists there. I wanted to be where there was real life. College was like my home life, all these very healthy girls went to bed at ten o'clock. So I came to Barnard College and Greenwich Village, let's see, about 1912.

"Oh, but I should say, too, that after graduation I worked one year on a newspaper in Minneapolis, and then I went to Europe. I saved my money and announced to my father, 'I'm going to Europe.' That was just before the war, in 1914. My poor father! I said, 'I have three hundred dollars. I'm going,' and he said, 'It's so dangerous.' But anyway he had to give me more money because he said, 'You can't do it on three hundred dollars.' So we went to Europe, a friend and I, and the war broke out. We went to France pretending we were refugees going in the wrong direction: 'We want to get to Paris.' But that was difficult, so I came back in steerage, which cost thirty-five dollars, and I had a lot of money left. So I just stayed in New York in Greenwich Village.

"I persuaded my father: 'Seriously, I'd love to study art. I can draw to beat the band.' Of course, I never did any work at all, I mean I was having too much fun. I didn't work at all, but went to Columbia and to the Independent Art School. I imagine it was a delayed and a very important time. You can't study when you're so full of interest and life and exuberance, isn't that true? and especially with this sort of delayed interest in the opposite sex. There's too much doing in your mind, too many jokes, you see.

"But I was exaggerating about being the great queen of Greenwich Village. The queen of Greenwich Village—I'm afraid that's a little hyperbolic. Just a jovial, nice girl, that's what being the queen was, but I imagine fun to talk to. I was absolutely exuberant, and New York was so much fun. I never could bear to ask my darling father for enough money, though. So I just had one suit, a blue serge suit, and no gloves and no coat. When I was outdoors, I was fine: I just ran. I was a tremendous long-distance runner. Imagine me running up Fifth Avenue. They don't know you're running, they think you're catching a perpetual bus. I was feeling how wonderful it is to be young. What tirelessness, what bounce.

"Greenwich Village was an awfully nice, darling place. Just think, there'd be a snowstorm and no cars and just nice, jolly, interesting people and lots of wonderful mad eggs down there.

I was the first one to have my hair cut off. Off, I mean short. Irene Castle had it somewhat short, down to her shoulders. Well, I went into Henri's at the Brevoort Hotel and said, 'Off, I want my hair off.' I had very nice black hair, and he said, 'How?'

" 'Like Lord Byron.' And then I explained, 'Cut it like a high wind is blowing from the rear.' So he cut it all off, and I got rid of that crowning glory but I felt so fine. I suppose it was a splendid attention-getting thing to do. Everyone else wore it very long with lots of combs, a regular edifice. So I had it nice and short and blowing, and I began to have lots of beaux.

"I had a roommate, Anne. She must have been twenty-three, not more. She had an English beau, and we had an apartment in Jane Street for nine dollars a month, a railroad flat. We had to break the ice to get a bath: cold water. It was so cold! We had the stove in the front room, which was way up front, and I think I was the first one to ever paint a kitchen black—with orange curtains, I remember that.

"Anne had a beau, and since my bedroom was next to where our parlor, so-called, was, I just knew from that low giggling and that low silence that they were—we didn't say necking— spooning, kissing. 'How can you be so ridiculous?' I thought. So that's not exactly like the present, is it?

"It was a walkup, four floors. We walked up stairs, up stairs, up stairs, and we built our own fire. I can remember going to bed and my roommate laughing because we always dressed for bed so we'd be warm. It was so cold, I think we even put the rug on us. I remember Anne dressing and saying, 'If there's going to be a fire, I don't want to miss it.'

"Well, now," Brenda Ueland said, taking a deep breath. Then she began again: "By that time, to stop being so fat, you know what I had done? There was a great Norwegian professor in Minneapolis and he had said, 'You must walk.' I lived on the lake four miles from town, and after college, when I worked on the newspaper, I walked downtown and back every day, eight miles a day. Instead of feeling lazy, I really began to feel better. I kept that up in New York and, of course, lost a few pounds. I walked from Greenwich Village to Columbia every day. It's only six miles, takes you an hour and a half, but that was quite interesting, too. I got to know all the policemen, almost every policeman in New York. I'd stop along when I could in a doorway and smoke, you see. Of course, I'd be arrested if they saw me. It wasn't against the law, no, but a woman, a *woman* doing it was simply a sight.

"Then sometimes I would walk downtown to Wall Street and to the New York *World* and across Brooklyn Bridge and back to Greenwich Village. That was one of my walks, too. Sometimes I would walk from Washington Square to Fifty-ninth Street and back. I had this compulsion: 'I've got to walk an hour and a half a day, be outdoors, or I will get lazy.'

"I remember I had the most wonderful apples in New York on my walks, and they haven't had such apples since then. They were called Spitzenburgs, and they cost three for a dime. I ate those all the time. About that: there was a short-story writer named Samuel Merwin, a rather round-faced man who was writing for a magazine. He knew my roommate, and one day he saw me crossing a street in Greenwich Village. I stood talking to him with one foot on the curb, eating an apple, and he put that in a story, this 'Greenwich Villager and the apples.' The illustrator even drew a picture of me to illustrate the story. Greenwich Village fascinated Merwin, you see."

I asked Miss Ueland if she had thought of herself as a bohemian. She considered the question in two ways. First, "No, I think we had very good manners. We were very considerate children." Then she added, "We were all free souls, my friends and I. People were getting freer then, protesting, but there was no blackguardism in this protest; rather, a great rising of socialism in the country. Bernard Shaw was in England, and the Fabians; and here there were young speechmaking socialists in Carnegie Hall.

"Labor was simply a horror. Men worked for nothing. My sister had seen the terrible fire in the Triangle Building, which was full of girls on the top floor who worked for a shirtwaistmaker. I think they made three dollars a week, if that, for twelve hours a day. Just incredible. Then there was a shirtwaist strike, and these girls were locked in. The boss wanted them to work harder, and bosses could do almost anything to any working person they wanted to. So, at this terrible Triangle fire, the girls were locked in the building and they burned to death. Of course, there was such injustice to females. For instance, we would go to night court and see a poor little prostitute sentenced to jail. She was pulled into night court, but her partners, oh no. They were only fined.

"There was the idea that working people were supposed to kill themselves for rich people because rich people were so splendid, but we were beginning to disagree. In Greenwich Village there were leaders like John Reed and Max Eastman, and *The Masses* was a wonderful, fiery, socialist magazine. There was Hippolyte Havel, who was an anarchist. Anarchism as a philosophy had been taking hold in Europe and Russia some years before it had an influence here. Then, of course, we began reading Tolstoy and other writers. Before the war there were suffragettes in London, and pretty soon, here, too."

Had she ever marched with the suffragettes?

"Oh, every time, all the time," she said. "There were such wonderful suffrage parades in New York, year after year. It was interesting. At the first one there were rowdies and catcalls and I think only about ten men dared to march in it. But we did. I remember one famous parade, John Reed used to tell about that one. There were hoodlums who poked sticks in our faces and yelled: 'You terrible women!' John Reed and some young radicals grabbed a lot of weapons from these hoodlums. He might have been attacked by them, but then he could mingle with the parade and march on uptown and get away from them.

"As the parades got better later on, they were very moving. There were nurses, professors and fine, wonderful women like Jane Addams. At first, the marchers were almost all women. Very beautiful, fashionable, brilliant women began to be in favor of suffrage. Some few extraordinarily fine men, like Mr. James Laidlaw, joined. Charles Beard, many great intellectuals, were fiercely for suffrage, and Eugene Debs, a great socialist, of course, who went to jail.

"I've never been in jail, to my regret," Miss Ueland said parenthetically. "Actually I was anxious to be arrested so I could get some reading done." She admonished: "You know, nobody writes unless they go to jail. You'll probably never be a great writer because you'll never get arrested. Think of Dostoevsky and Socrates and Bunyan. You must try to get arrested for a noble cause. It's easy. It's easier to get arrested for a noble cause, you know, than for a murder."

Then she began to talk about the Greenwich Villagers she had known. "There was a famous character named Griffin Barry. Griffin Barry was charming, wistful; he looked like Eros, lovely face. Well, Griffin Barry seemed to like me, he liked everybody. He came in one night—I had a ground-floor apartment and never would think of locking a door—and said someone was staying where he lived with his friend, 'So I'm going to stay here all night.' Well, I was naturally hospitable. I wasn't the kind of society dame who would pull herself up to her full height and say: 'Sir, be gone.' So I said, 'Sleep over there, go on,' but it affronted me terribly. I didn't care about my good name, it wasn't that, but it was an offensive bohemianism that I didn't like. Heavens, I could have licked him— given him the old one-two! But I remember playing the mouth organ all night—I had been practicing on the mouth organ— and he finally got up from sleeplessness. I think he left about five in the morning. I drove him out with my mouth organ.

"Then I met another beau at a party, an interesting party. There was a beautiful, wonderful woman, a writer, Mary Heaton Vorse, who gave the party. She was bohemian but bohemian with money, a house and a maid. She gave quite a grand party. There were a lot of eminent people there— Hutchins Hapgood, Norman Hapgood, Amos Pinchot. Big Bill Haywood of the I.W.W. was there too, a one-eyed man, a great labor leader, wonderful man. Rich New Yorkers, and I went to the party in my sole garment, my blue suit.

"There was a man there, a handsome, youngish man. His name was Bayard Boyesen, and he was a professor at Columbia. Philosophically, he was an anarchist, but he was a very rich man who had a great farm in Massachusetts and horses. He looked quite Hellenic, curly-haired. He had a Norse face because he was half Norwegian, you see, and I'm half Norwegian, too. He seemed to fall in love with me, or whatever you call it, and said, 'Your face is very Norse, very Norse.' Well, I didn't think so, *but*. He wore a chocolate-brown suit with a flame-colored tie. There was a note of Oscar Wilde elegance, too. He said he wanted to come and see me: 'Well, why don't you?'

"So I remember he came to Jane Street, up the stairs, with

Hutchins Hapgood who had a thunderous, wonderful voice. So here was Bayard Boyesen calling on me, think of that! I was very elated. It was quite a conquest.

"Well, he came to see me a few times. And once my shirt was open at the throat, and I was sort of tanned, sort of sunburned there. He sat on this army cot next to me, and then he leaned over and kissed me on the throat. 'Well,' I said, 'that's very fine for you, I mean, emotionally. But I don't feel a thing.' Then I felt embarrassed. 'But what am I supposed to do now?' I said. At which he got up and paced up and down like Hamlet, clasping his hands behind him. 'Oh, to think of it!' was his reaction, as though I had torn him to pieces with despair.

"Well, for a while he became a kind of a beau, and I was very much interested. I was very elated, but he wasn't any fun. He was one of those men that when you talk, a kind of asbestos curtain comes down. They're only interested in talking themselves, you see. But I remember telling friends, in a jokey way, that he wanted me to shout from the housetops, 'I love you illicitly. I love you illicitly.'

"Well, it never came about because I had a very interesting and, I think, a good sense of honor. My parents wouldn't have liked it, and I felt that since my father was sending me fifty dollars a month, well, I couldn't do it. If I made my own money, I thought I could do anything I wanted to. I believe there's a logic to that: are you going to stand by your own scalligwaginess, you know, or not. Well, that was Bayard Boyesen. He went to Greece, and we wrote some elaborate letters for a while, and then he married another person.

"I was awfully happy in Greenwich Village, awfully happy, and then after a while I fell in love with a person, not the right person probably, and married. He was divorced and I had to help him get a divorce. Fierce devotion between us, I mean fierce devotion. He was older than I, and of course, as in many cases, he married me, I didn't marry him. You know how it is: 'How nice of you!' I always say that, I remind myself of the girl who, when someone called her up and said, 'Nancy, will you marry me?' said, 'Of course, I will. Who is this talking?' Well, I was born to be uncalculating, and I have always felt that way. I can't stand plan-iness or putting yourself forward for the wrong reason."

I was reminded of Miss Ueland's autobiography, which is called simply, *Me*. "That's a straightforward book," I said.

"Oh yes, it is," she answered. "In fact, perhaps it's the only straightforward book ever written. But don't read that. Read something good. Read the Bible or Shakespeare, Yeats and Blake."

But when pressed, she did talk about *Me*: "I wrote that in 1938, when I had been divorced and had a child. I don't know why I should write a biography, because my life isn't of any real importance, but I had a theory about writing. I taught a writing class once in Minneapolis, and I found that I could turn my students into geniuses. I used to say, 'When you write what you really think, it's interesting. As soon as it comes from you, it's alive.' For instance, some little person in my class might say, 'I saw the robin.' Well, if she saw the robin, it was interesting. But other times I would say, 'This sentence is no good. In this sentence, you're thinking of teacher, you're thinking of me. It's no good at all.' I mean, always write impulsively.

"So that was just the way I wrote that book. I got a commission to do it, and I type as fast as I think, and I wrote a million words or more, everything I could remember, everything on paper. Then I'd begin again. There was a system of sloughing off; slough off the boring, garrulous, fake. Sometimes I'd be writing that book and I'd get stuck. Then I'd think, 'Why am I stuck? Because you're trying to lie! You're trying to be pretty, to be effective.' Well then, I'd say in the book, 'I seem to be wanting to lie to you now.' I think that's probably the secret. Most autobiographies are a little arranged—'dear little episodes'—a kind of string of pearls that doesn't really tell you who they are.

"Now I don't know who I am. We are all mysterious, but still that book would be who I am, whether bad or good or whatever. So in that way I think it has some virtue.

"I'm what you would call a Renaissance man. In the Renaissance they spoke of the universal man. I'm universal because I think you have to be poly-minded or it's no good. I don't think you can feel good-natured and I don't think you can feel fearless unless you feel happy and strong. All this tramp, tramp to the psychiatrists! I know myself how to be well. Health is like freedom, it's won every day, you know. A lady once asked me, 'What will you do when you really do get sick? What will you do?' 'I'll kick the bucket,' I said.

"Walk and move and work and sweat; walk, be alone, and talk to the Lord, you know. Find out yourself, look inward and outward both. You have to find your center and live from that, if you can, and your center may change every day. For instance, I don't know whether I'm a burglar or a grandee or an archangel or an old slob. You're all those things, but let them come to life if they feel like it and then try to understand each phase."

I asked how she felt about young people today. She was of two minds. (In *Me,* she has written that she is often torn between generosity, kindness and a grim spirit which is much more Spartan.) "I think young people today are adorable and wonderful," she began. "I'm sure they are much better than we were.

"It's hard to know, but I think there is also a kind of physical deterioration. Girls today, you could extinguish them with your thumb and forefinger. They have no strength at all. For instance, I like to walk early in the morning. I walk around the lake, maybe go six miles. The boys are out running, little high-school boys practicing track, but there's not a girl even walking.

"In my youth, we used to swim, but now you go down to the beach and they're putting on suntan oil and not anyone can swim. As a girl, I got to be the most wonderful swimmer. The lake was about a mile and a half across, and I can now swim overhand across the lake and back, an old lady. Sure I can, though I must say I haven't done it for the last two summers. But I like to say to people in my boastful way, 'I give a standing challenge to any man or woman, from the age of one to ninety-nine, to race me across Lake Calhoun and back.' Then I say, 'But you've got to build a grandstand first. Unless I have a grandstand for people to watch, I won't do it.'" She laughed.

"Well then, young people today. I think they have become centripetal. They want things towards them, they don't want to go out. But heavens, I can't judge. I've seen this dancing on TV, that violent dancing, and I think it's fascinating. But they should perhaps be outdoors more. People are a little too rich now, so that nobody moves an inch. I mean, it took us five million years to develop legs to move. Otherwise we're like trees. Legs are the most wonderful things that exist. Nobody uses them.

"I walk so far every day because I think that nobody has any solitude at all, and if you're walking you can't sew or read and you're bound to have something reflective. But if you're busy all the time and have that ishy accomplishment compulsion—for dinky work, ridiculous work, doily carrying—you don't have solitude. That's why I think working people and physical people, who work with their bodies, have a deep kindness—the salt of the earth, and the heart is a muscle, you know. Gandhi was asked, 'What do you think is worst about modern times?' 'The hardheartedness of the intellectual,' he said. So now, about women for example, think of us women letting our little boys of eighteen go and kill and fight. We shouldn't allow it for one second, or we should do it ourselves.

"Walking is what all saints experience, forty days in the wilderness. We should have that all the time. When I'm walking, ideas come—not always, and I don't expect it always, but I work on it. You're above your ordinary self then. Compared to that, the psychiatrist is just hocus-pocus. Not experiencing that, the openness, more often is nobody's fault. It's the fault of nervous distraction.

"Distraction. I've seen it happen. I have a friend, or did years ago. She was a beautiful blond angel, adorable. She was divorced and she wanted to write. Her house was in New Canaan, mine was in Stamford, and we were great friends. She, unfortunately for her, had more money than I did, and she never would write. She put it off all the time. She would say, 'Well, you see, Brenda, I can't now. I just am going to—well, I haven't got the spinach ready. I have to have a maid.' Imagine a man talking that way! Imagine Ernest Hemingway saying, 'I can't write because I haven't got the spinach ready.' So apply this test to yourself. Test yourself against great heroes, you as a female. Don't accept something dim and very lazy and cowardly, as our silly sex does.

"More distractions—drinking and smoking. Well, of course, I used to smoke, but I don't now. I do take a drink, but it's really no good. I don't think of myself as a teetotaler, but I am speaking now in terms of athletics. I'm in training, you see. I prefer vigor. With drinking, you knock your brains out. It's absolutely true. There is a great essay by Tolstoy called 'Why Men Stupefy Themselves'—you must read that sometime. We want to be knocked out because then we haven't responsibility or a hint of courage. The hardest thing in life is making decisions. When you're knocking yourself out, you don't worry about it at all, you stay in the groove. The drinkers all stay in their groove. They never have the courage to do anything else. And when you don't smoke, you have a third more energy. When you smoke, you're both nervous and lazy at the same time, but when you don't, you want to act, not talk. Say you're in a night club and you are smoking and drinking. You could sit there till five in the morning. Otherwise, you couldn't stand it five minutes, you'd go home, read William James and go to bed."

She spoke with gusto, suggesting, as her autobiography does, that the stamina of the suffragettes had always been more than a social issue to her. As a girl, she wanted to be knightly, not a fainting violet. She still feels that. "Women should be more manly, and men should be far more womanly, much more tender and much more graceful, beautiful. I mean, women should neither be subordinate nor superior. We should all be wonderful creatures, gods and goddesses. To do that, you see, you have to have a vision of what it would be. It isn't just do it, but see what you think is wonderful and then *love* it. Don't say, 'I've got to do it' and set your jaw, but love it and see it and it will happen."

Mrs. Lyndon Baines Johnson

Claudia Alta Taylor Johnson was born on December 22, 1912, in an historic brick house on the outskirts of Karnack, in east Texas. Built in the 1850's, the house was a pleasant, comfortable place with nine large rooms. Claudia was the baby of the family and the only girl; a nursemaid gave her the nickname of "Lady Bird." Her brother, Tom, Jr., was eleven years older and Tony, her second brother, was eight years older.

Her father, Thomas Jefferson Taylor, who operated a general store, was active in other businesses, too; and in Karnack, he was known as "Mr. Boss." Her mother, Minnie Patillo Taylor of Alabama, loved reading to her, and Mrs. Johnson still remembers how marvelous it seemed that her mother could produce such wonderful stories from the little black marks on the pages of books.

Just before her sixth birthday her mother died and thereafter she was cared for by her mother's sister, Aunt Effie Patillo. "Perhaps I had a lonely childhood, but it didn't seem lonely to me," she recalls. During the summer her aunt would take her back to Alabama to visit their Patillo relatives.

She went to Fern School, a one-room schoolhouse down the road from the Taylor home, and attended high school in Jefferson, Texas (during the school year she lived with her Aunt Effie), and in Marshall, Texas. A girl of quick intelligence, she graduated at fifteen. She recalls that being younger than the rest of the high-school students was not an advantage. For one thing, she was shy, and "I used to hope no one would speak to me."

After high school, too young to start at the University of Texas, she went instead to an Episcopal girls' school in Dallas, St. Mary's. Two years later, she enrolled at the University in Austin, where she took a B.A. in liberal arts and a B.J. in journalism; at the same time she was busy earning a teaching certificate and studying shorthand and typing. She had not yet completely conquered her shyness. Told that she was to be awarded the valedictory medal, she had her grades adjusted downwards to avoid making the necessary speech.

When she met Lyndon Baines Johnson in 1934, he was twenty-six years old and had his first Washington job, as secre-

tary to Texas Congressman Richard M. Kleberg. Two months later he proposed and they were married.

Throughout Lyndon Johnson's career as Congressman, Senator, Vice-President and President, Mrs. Johnson has been closely involved in his activities. In 1942, he went to war in the Pacific, and she worked in his congressional office—answering mail from "the folks back home."

Since then she has increasingly developed a political personality and significance of her own. In 1960, when Lyndon Johnson was running for the vice-presidency, she took a course in public speaking, and proved herself a charming and effective campaigner for her husband. There was no doubt that she had mastered her earlier fears of facing an audience. "Thousands of barbecues and hundreds of speeches helped," she says. "Lyndon expects a lot of me, and I've learned not to be afraid any more."

As First Lady, Mrs. Johnson has been particularly interested in the President's Program on Recreation and Natural Beauty, and has thrown the full weight of her prestige and energy into promoting it. She has continued Mrs. Jacqueline Kennedy's efforts to preserve and enhance the historic White House, and has, as well, made additions especially to interest the nation's schoolchildren and other visitors to the capitol.

Her efficiency is not limited to politics. In 1943, for example, with an inheritance from the settlement of her mother's estate, she purchased an Austin radio station, KTBC. Mrs. Johnson took an active interest in its management until 1963 when, during her husband's tenure as President, KTBC was placed in the hands of trustees.

With all this activity, Mrs. Johnson has remained first of all a wife and mother. Lynda Bird, born in 1944, and Luci Baines, born in 1947, have not grown up as the children of a working woman too busy to spend time with them. On the contrary, Lady Bird Johnson thinks of herself as a homemaker. A woman's "first and most important business," she has said, "is to provide a comfortable, peaceful, efficient, and above all a happy home."

One of the nicest compliments Lady Bird Johnson (called "Bird" by her friends and family) has received came from Sam Rayburn, the late Speaker of the House. "That is the greatest woman I've ever known," he said. "She's good and she's kind. She hasn't a mean thought, and she's got more sense than most men. The smartest thing Lyndon ever did was to marry her. He's just lucky."

Mrs. Lyndon Baines Johnson

M<small>RS.</small> J<small>OHNSON</small> is waiting for us," Liz Carpenter said in a soft Texas accent as she greeted me. "We'll go right over."

Mrs. Carpenter, a jolly, gray-haired woman who is Mrs. Lyndon Johnson's Press Secretary, led the way out of her office in the East Wing of the White House. We went down corridors past groups of officials, visitors and an occasional White House policeman, then took an elevator from which we emerged at the stairs leading to the second floor of the White House. On this floor are the President's living quarters, as well as a number of state rooms not open to the public.

At the top of the stairs, sitting at a small table, a man who might have been a Secret Service agent said that Mrs. Johnson was with the President. Mrs. Carpenter escorted me down a wide hall, away from the West, or living, end of the White House. On either side were notable rooms—the Yellow Oval Room, the Treaty Room, the Lincoln Bedroom. Some of the doors were open, and I saw elegant, carefully placed furniture on great expanses of carpeting and polished wood floors. Through a window, I caught a glimpse of the Washington Monument to the south.

Our destination was a room at the very end of the hall, the Queen's Sitting Room, adjacent to the Queen's Bedroom, so named because visiting royal women—Elizabeth II of Great Britain, Frederika of Greece and Wilhelmina and Juliana of the Netherlands—have stayed in it.

Mrs. Johnson appeared—smiling—and apologized for being late. She sat facing me across a small dark wood table. She looks younger than she does in photographs and her face has a softness and delicacy that are sometimes lost to the camera. Her deep blue dress, decorated with an enameled pin of the American flag, contrasted with the brighter blue of the room's wallpaper.

"Well," she said, "it's very pleasant to think back to my sixteenth year. That was a very special time. I remember sixteen as a time of feeling intensely alive. It was like a butterfly breaking out of its chrysalis. I think there is never a time when the world seems so full of delight, when the sun shines so brightly, the cypress tree is more delicately green, the orange trumpet vine more vibrant in color. And one's feelings are so alive to it all, so heightened to the promise and beauty of the world.

"Then also, at sixteen I was being exposed to some very bright minds, and that had great importance for me. That year I had the good fortune to have a wonderful English teacher who made words and putting together phrases a source of excitement. Ever since, it has made me reach for something better in reading and writing, made me more aware of what beauty can be expressed in words.

"I was attending a girls' Episcopal boarding school then. Of course, there is a certain stark loneliness in all boarding schools, unmatched for someone as shy as I. I'm sure the other girls there felt this loneliness too. Yet, I did make some close friends whom I still enjoy seeing.

"When I look back on it, that was what might be called the 'time of the iconoclast.' We were being exposed to so much that was new, ideas and history, presented in a fresh way, so that we were forced to think differently about many things we thought we were familiar with.

"Sixteen was also my introduction to the theater. The school believed—and I think it was a good thing—in exposing us to the arts, and they would load us in a bus and take us to the theater in Dallas. I really fell in love with the theater for life as a result of that. I remember, we saw so many plays! There was the science fiction of *R-U-R*, which had a great sociological undercurrent, and *They Knew What They Wanted*, a warm, humorous, painful play which I thought was enthralling. And I remember the Ferenc Molnar play, what was it?"—Mrs. Johnson pondered for an instant—"*Carousel*, no, it was called *Liliom* then. When it was made into a musical, they changed the title to *Carousel*.

"Because of this intellectual awareness that began for me in boarding school, I was determined that I'd offer my children the same opportunity. I tried to have a hand in their education and to direct them to people who would stir their minds. I think Lynda Bird got this at the University of Texas, for instance.

"Of course my own experience was quite different from my daughters'. I don't really think I was typical at sixteen. I had grown up way out in the country. My mother was dead and my father was very much involved in his business. I was raised by a gentle aunt, and she was a wonderful influence on my life in a purely non-material way, teaching me to love walking in the woods and to read omnivorously. She did not help me select clothes or plan parties or arrange little visits with other, 'suitable' children. Such practical direction of life was alien to her, and consequently, in retrospect, I'm sure my childhood appeared very lonely to others. Actually, *I* never thought so. I went to a one-room grade school, in which there were perhaps fifteen children, and when I came home from school, I was free to play or do whatever I liked. We lived in a great big white-columned, red-brick house that was built before the Civil War. (There was a legend that it was haunted!) It was a wonderful place and I loved it.

"I really did enjoy my childhood tremendously. It wasn't the practical sort of upbringing that many parents arrange for children, perhaps. I was probably more independent than many children are. But what I had, I loved, and it shaped my life quite happily, I think."

I asked Mrs. Johnson if she could compare her childhood with what young people today experience.

"I certainly didn't grow up with a great cluster of friends who did everything together," she said, "but there were social events and young people around. One begins to reach for people at sixteen, I think. I would have my cousins come and spend a week of the summer with me in Texas. Then I would visit them in Alabama. My mother's family was from Alabama, and I had been going to Alabama every summer since I was five years old. Then later, there were visits from the girls at St. Mary's."

"When you had a friend visit," I asked, "what did you do for fun?"

Mrs. Johnson's eyes are a deep brown, warm and expressive. They sparkled now as she said: "I do remember one kind of party we would go on that was fun—a houseparty, on the banks of Caddo Lake in east Texas, where we would fish, swim and tell tales under the starlight. We would paddle small bateaus through lagoons lined with cypress trees, where Spanish moss hung to the water. Occasionally we would see turtles lined up on the logs, and sometimes we heard a mysterious splash and imagined it was an alligator slithering into the water!" She laughed at her jungle imagery.

Then, pausing in thought for a moment, she said, "I recall one important thing that happened to me when I was just turning sixteen. It had a strong effect on my feelings toward my father, and later, toward my own children. I had graduated from high school and decided to go to an Episcopal girls' school in Dallas before going on to the University of Texas. My father surprised me by taking a trip to see the school. He concluded that it wasn't a good choice, and he told me so. Actually, he was right. After I'd been there for a while, I came to realize what he meant. It wasn't a vital school in many ways—though I did tap rich veins there and I'm glad I went. But when my father told me he didn't think too highly of the school, I stubbornly said: 'I think it's right for me,' and he said: 'That's fine. I want you to make up your own mind.' I respected him very much for that.

"I hope I've practiced the same philosophy with my own children. I've tried to let Luci and Lynda Bird know that they are trusted as to judgment and character, and I've left them considerable leeway, because I feel that children are likely to live up to what you believe of them. But there is a place for positive discipline—and I think it is something that children want, something that makes them feel cherished when they have it, and lonely and abandoned when it isn't in the background of their lives. The greatest satisfaction I've had as a parent has been to see the lessons I've tried to impart—and thought had been ignored—blossom forth, sometimes years later, in one of the children."